the LIVING WATERS of JOY

The LIVING WATERS of JOY

HEAL YOUR SOUL IN HIS PRESENCE

GRACE LUCIA KIMBALL

Radiant Books
New York

The Living Waters of Joy was originally published anonymously as *Living Waters or Messages of Joy* in 1919. Illustrated by Vinegarice.

Illustrations © 2023 by Radiant Books

Library of Congress Control Number: 2023951161

Published in 2023 by Radiant Books
radiantbooks.co

ISBN 978-1-63994-045-5 (hardback)
ISBN 978-1-63994-046-2 (paperback)
ISBN 978-1-63994-047-9 (e-book)

CONTENTS

Note *vii*

The First Message **1**

The Second Message **69**

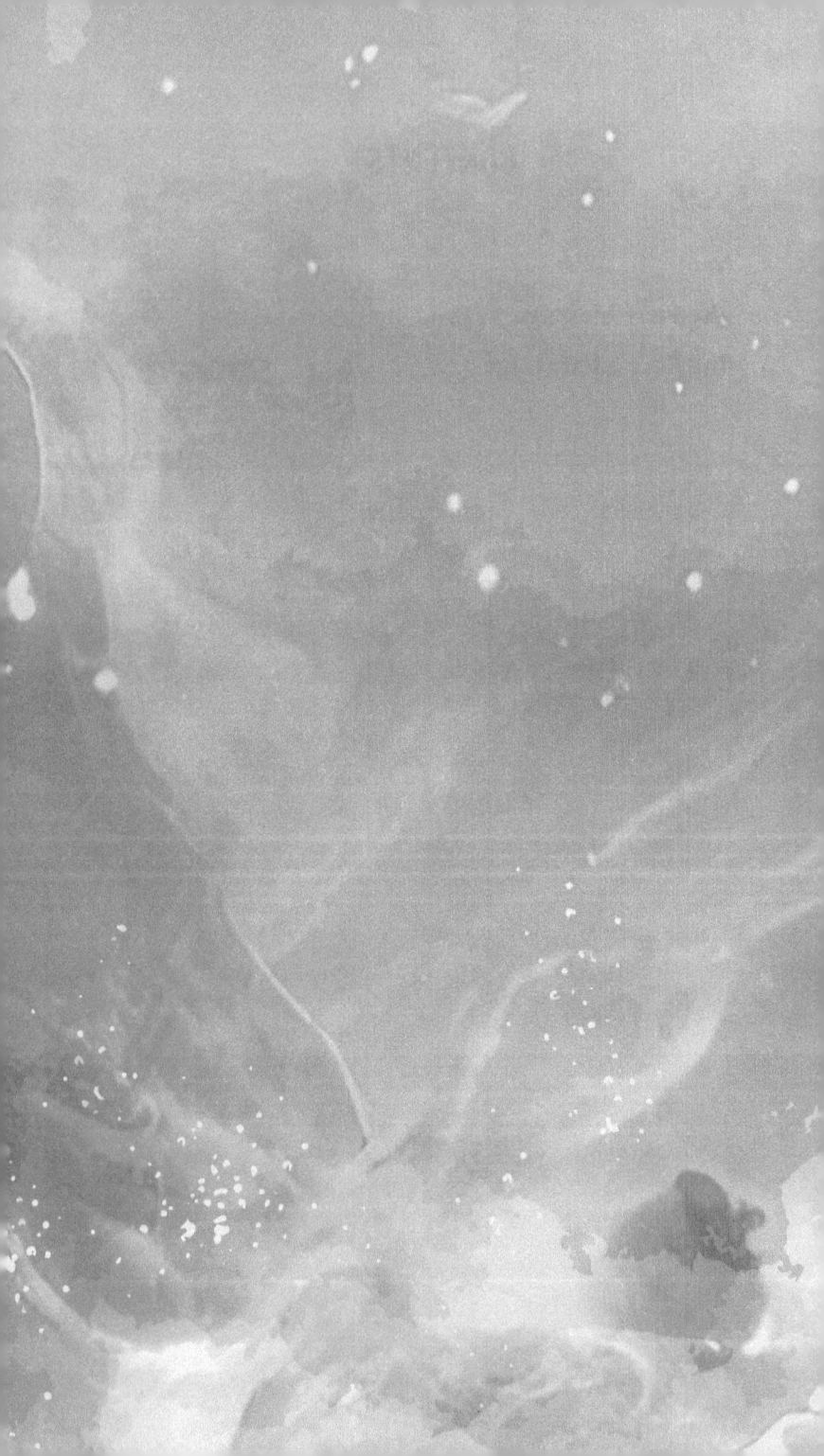

NOTE

These messages were spoken to me by the "still, small voice" that speaks in all men. The voice that I heard spoke in my breast, not in my head, and the words dropped one by one, so that each sentence was taken on faith, as it were, until it was finished. I wrote the words down as they came, and they usually came as fast as I could write. The spacing, as printed, between the writing of any given day, indicates short periods of time — a minute or two or three — during which the voice was silent.

The messages began one day when I sat down to do some writing connected with the work in which I was then engaged. I was alone at the time, and for the succeeding two or three days, I was alone when I took down the messages. After that, I wrote in the presence of a friend. Not a word has been changed.

To me these writings are the answer to a pervading desire that, I think I may say, had become the strongest desire of my life: the desire to know more of the laws and the life of the spirit. There was nothing so intensely interesting to me as the spiritual realm toward which the human race is slowly but surely advancing.

For me, and for those who have followed them, these messages have meant instruction in the unfolding of that incredibly simple law of faith which was stated so perfectly by Jesus Christ when He said: "Therefore I say unto you, What things soever ye desire, when ye pray, believe that ye receive them, and ye shall have them."

But most of all, these messages have given me a steadfast consciousness of the reality of God as a loving Presence, who never leaves us, who never fails us, whose mighty wisdom works out the smallest detail of our daily lives, and whose power, the one and only, brings unto all men, who persistently seek it and lovingly yield to it, an ever-increasing freedom from limitations and a joyous and thankful sense of partnership in all the riches of the Spiritual Kingdom.

The one who received the messages

the FIRST MESSAGE

1919

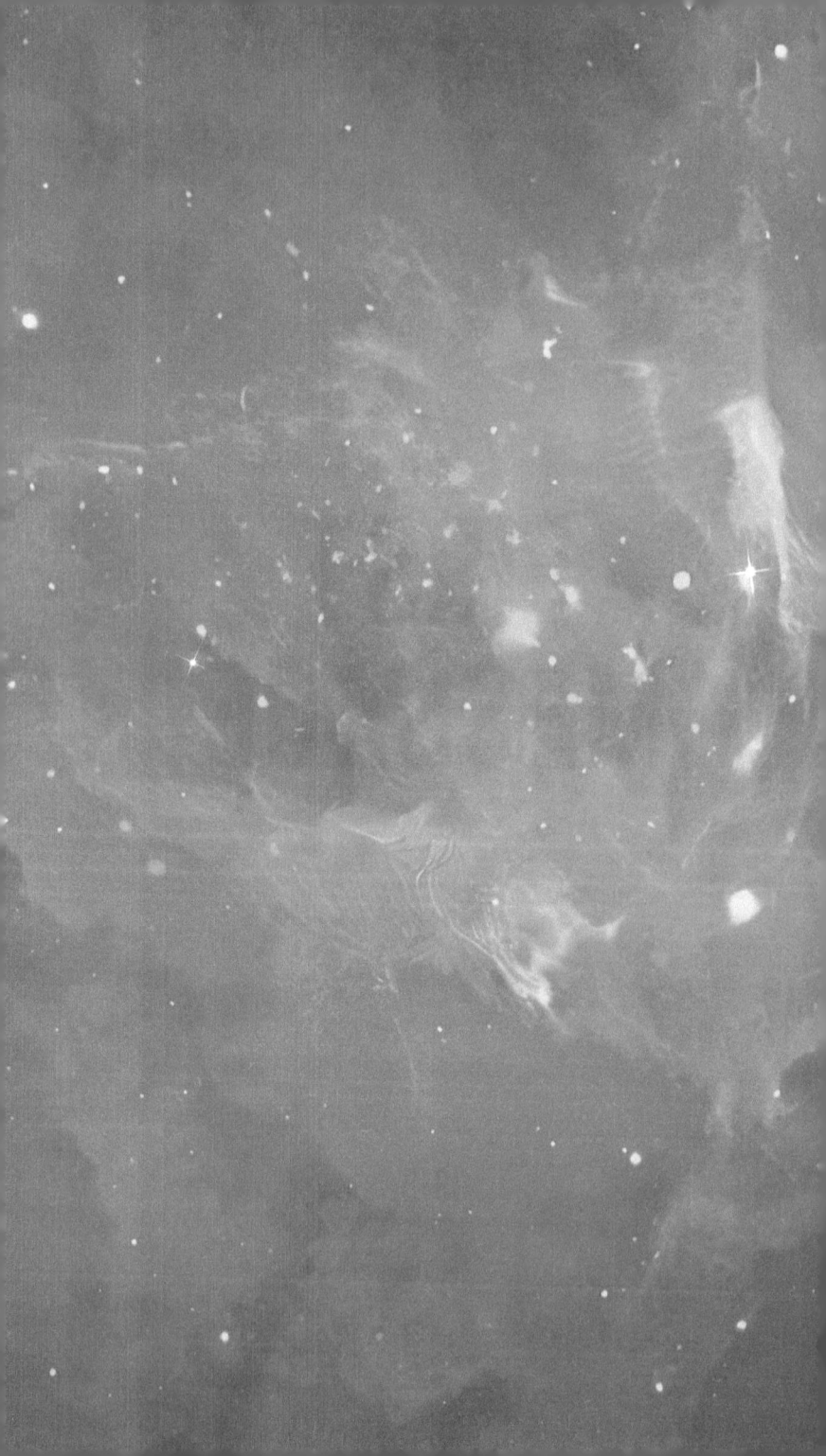

THE FIRST MESSAGE

February 21

Speak thou the words that I shall set down. Listen to the words that I shall utter. Faith has no measure of the words that I shall speak. Earth has no knowledge of the words that are Mine. I speak in a language that has no reason, for reason is man's proof of what he does not understand. What I shall say is what I see with My eyes, what I shall tell you is what I know from the works of God. There is not reason in life, there is only life. Seek ye the source.

I have come that all men should know what I know, that all men should take what has been theirs from the beginning of the world. I am the I that is in all men. Men know Me not because they know not that they are one with Me who was from the beginning.

What I say to you, I say to all men. Spread the word that I shall give, the sacred, common word that lies hidden in all hearts. Receive thou Me. When all has been made light, then shall you know what the light hides with its brightness, even the God upon whom you cannot now bear to look.

Judge not My words. Think not. Set them down.

～

On the seventh day there came riding into the city, a man on a white ass, a little ass with a tail like a hempen rope. And the man said to them that followed after him, "What seek ye?" And they answered, "Thou, O Lord God of Israel."

Then answered he, "Seek ye me in that place where no man meets aught but himself."

And they marveled, saying, "What meaneth he? How can a man meet another in that place where he meets no one but himself? And where is that place? Where go we that no other comes?"

But he who sat upon the white ass only smiled, as was his habit, and said, "Seek ye my meaning in your hearts. And say to him whom thou shalt meet there, that I am come, even he who was there from the beginning."

And again they marveled and left him not, for he drew them after him as a strong man draweth in his nets heavy with fish.

So it came to pass on that day that he passed through the city of Tirzah, that a man came to him crying, "Lord, I have sought you from afar, from afar have I cried unto you. Why turnest thou away?"

And he that rode upon the white ass said, "Turn I from you? Can a man turn away from himself, or a hungry man from the bread he breaks? Know you not that I have sought you from the beginning, and you come crying, 'Why turnest thou away, O Lord?'

"Turn thou, and thou shalt find me, even thou thyself shalt find me myself, and God shall fold us one with another and breathe the breath of His healing into us twain until no man can say whether I turn to bless you or you, running, hasten to bless me with thy withered hand that now is made whole."

And it was in that moment even so as he said; and the man raised the hand that had been made whole and blessed him who rode through the city on a white ass, a little white ass with a tail like a hempen rope.

And so it was that wherever he went there ran after him multitudes crying to be healed, and he healed them all, for their need was great. Great was their need in that day and great was their blessing.

Great is thy need today and great shall be thy blessing.

THE FIRST MESSAGE

Turn not from My voice. Doubt not. Receive Me.

Now is the time to speak in the voice of one who knows and doubts not. Can I not speak, think you, because I am no longer in the flesh beside you? Beloved, I died on the cross that I might speak to all men.

Doubt never. Thrust your hand into My side. Prove Me what I am. Love Me and be filled. Need I not you, as I need all men?

I and the Father and all His children are bound together in one body, a body of love.

Receive thou Me.

~

And he spake in this wise, saying, "There was a man who said unto his master, 'I have had naught from you but curses and hard blows. Now shall I take my wife and my children and the little goods that ever I have saved under thy scanty wages, and I shall go into a far country where there is no labor but that which the servant gives out of love to his master.'

"And he took his wife and his children and his goods and he went into that far country where a servant gives his labor unto his master out of the love that he bears him. And when he was come thither, lo, he was but at the further side of that which was his own land, over which ruled the hard master who had given him naught but curses and hard blows. And the master who came unto him was even he who had made his days heavy and his nights of no refreshment.

"But his countenance was shining with love so that his servant would have known him not except that he bore upon his forehead the sign of the master who ruled that land. And the servant said unto him, 'How find I you whom I sought to leave, and how, finding you, art thou so different?'

"And the master said, 'Am I then so different? Can the master be other than that the servant seeketh to find in him? Go back where thou comest from, even to thine own little roof that is lonely for thee under the stars, and there shalt thou find me even as thou findest me here, and thou shalt give me thy labor for love of me.'

"And the servant returned unto the roof that he had left, unto the land that he had tilled, and his master met him with loving words, even as he had met him afar; and the servant served him in love for he had found what he sought."

"What seek ye? Me?" saith the Lord.

February 25

These were the words He spake in the days He walked the earth. These are the words He speaks when He lies hidden in all men's hearts. Nothing shall be set down except in truth. Nothing shall be born but that which endureth. The time has come when every man shall listen within his own heart for the truth that God speaks to him.

The way to life is through the heart of man. Let each man seek himself in the silence of his own heart. There will he find his God and will talk with Him. This is prayer. Each man receives his own message, his own freedom, from the God whom he meets when he turns in faith to the quiet place in his own heart.

Let him turn each morning and listen. Let him turn each night and seek. Let him turn always, until he knows, as he knows the common outward things of life, that his God is ever with him, ever listening, ever answering, never failing.

Unto all men is the voice and the presence of a love that has no end. Unto all men is the message and the work, his work that he does in the confident joy of one who does work that he alone can do.

Seek and find. Listen and hear. Open and be filled. Receive and give. Peace be unto you.

⁓

And it came to pass upon that day that the mountain was moved from its roots and cast into the sea, that a man, who knew no manner of what he said for fear had taken all power of knowing from him, came into that temple that was left standing beside the shore of the sea, even that temple in which was preached the message of the Risen Christ.

And as the man fell trembling before the altar, a great light drew down about him, and a voice out of the light said, "Why hast thou sought Me here? Knowest thou not that I am even now knocking at the door of thy soul? Why fear ye and seek Me? Am I one to seek since it is I who never leave thee?"

And the man trembled and cried, "The mountain has cast itself into the sea at Thy command. How then can I not be full of the fear of Thy might?"

And the voice within the light shone round about him as the music of a thousand radiant souls, and he knew no more.

When he waked, it was nightfall, and there was no light in the temple, for the priests had fled with the rushing of the mountain into the sea. But the man stretched out his hand and touched the hand of another who lay beside him, and that other cried out, startled, for he had crept into the temple when the night had come and had not known that another lay beside him.

"Who art thou?" he cried in fear.

And he who had slept, answered, "Our God toucheth thee. Arise, let us go out hand in hand into the air."

And when they were come into the outer air, behold, each looked on the other, and they fell on each other's necks and laughed for joy, for they were brothers, long lost, who had nursed at the same breast.

"Where hast thou been, O my brother?" cried the one; and "Where hast thou been, O my brother?" cried the other. "Even now I sought you, on this very day when the mountain was cast into the sea."

"Even so didst thou? Then know that I, who lay beside thee in the temple, had been lying without the gates of thy house every night, longing to enter, fearing to knock. The mountain cast itself into the sea that I might cast myself into thy arms. For what cannot the longing of love bring to pass?"

And they embraced again and went forth to the house of him who had fled to the temple on that day when the mountain cast itself into the sea. And behold, the sea was calm, like a pond that mirrors clear stars, and in that place where the mountain had stood was a pool, deep as the mountain had been high, for even as the top is that which is hid.

Seek ye the hidden depths.

~

Now in this day I speak words that I have left until this day. I do not come to bring confusion and the sword. I come to bring the nearness of each man to his neighbor and his God.

The hour has come when all men shall know Me. I shall come to each man in the way that is his way, and the way of no other. Unto this man shall be the fruit of the vine that he has tended, and unto another the fruit that is his. All are branches of the one tree of life. Let no man think that he has no life to draw from the source and to give to his neighbor. All men are doers of the will of God.

THE FIRST MESSAGE

Now has come the time when there shall be no disputes, because men shall know that each man is doing the will of Him who sent him, even as I do the will of Him who sent Me. I and the Father are one. You and the Father are one. Fear not to call. Receive with a joyous heart. Let no man say, "I am not called." All men are called from the beginning.

Now is the day near when there shall appear in the sky the light of this, My Coming. And no man shall know that I am not come to part but to bring together all nations, for, in that hour, will all men have turned their hands one against another. I shall speak clearly in that day, and each man shall hear, and none shall know Me not who I am.

Now come to the feast while the table is spread and fill yourself. Open your belly to the words of God. Fill your heart with the joy of My Coming. And when I am with you in all openness, continue to seek, for then are you standing on the threshold, then are you but at the opening of the way. The way is the path to the God of your love. Follow and be folded in His arms, even as I am held in the bosom of His love.

~

Now in that day when the sun stopped in its course, a man stood in the marketplace crying that his wares were trampled under foot by the fearful feet of those who feared that the end of the world had come.

And as he cried, cursing, that his goods were despoiled, a voice out of the darkness cried, "Who art thou that thinkest of thy goods when all others are thinking of the day of judgment? Knowest thou not that a man and his wares are as nothing in that day when a man shall stand naked before his Maker?"

But he continued to curse and to feel about with his feet and hands for the goods that lay trampled by the hurrying heels of those who ran hither and thither, fearing that the end of the world was upon them.

Then as he felt the stones beneath him, a hand touched his hand and clung to him, grasping his ankles and smoothing his garment, and a voice said, "Why seek ye wares trampled in the dust and despoiled? Seek thou me."

And the merchant tried to free himself from the clinging hands, and he shook his garment loose and would have gone, but the hands clung the closer and the voice cried again, "What wares art thine but the love of thy soul for its God? Can aught else endure? Seek thou that before thou losest it in the heat of the marketplace."

And as the voice sounded, the sun came forth from the darkness that had hidden it and there was a strange glory in the light, and the glory came not from the sun but from the beggar that clung to the feet of the merchant, smoothing his garment.

And as the merchant looked, the glory faded, and the face was the face of the beggar who came every day, begging, at the opening of his stall, asking for a crust of kindness from him who sold only that which money can buy. And as the merchant looked, marveling, the beggar smiled, and throwing apart the rags that were his covering, he showed the merchant a hole in his side that was shining as with hidden treasure of great price.

"Didst thou think that I was poor, I, the beggar at thy gate? Behold the treasure that no man can take from me."

And he showed the man the treasure that lay hidden beneath the rags, deep within the clean hole in his side. And again the glory shone forth from the beggar and again the merchant marveled.

THE FIRST MESSAGE

"Canst thou trample on that which no man can take from me? Or curse the darkness when thy light is within thee? Open thy side and receive."

And the merchant felt his garment torn asunder over his heart, and a great hand that was strong and hot took out his heart and held it close and pressed it until a drop of blood flowed from it upon the rags of the beggar, and where it fell there sprang forth a tiny rose of exceeding sweetness.

Then did the hand put back the man's heart within his breast, and he looked about him, and behold, the beggar was no longer beside him, but from afar off, at the edge of the multitude that came surging back into the marketplace, was a glory going forth as of the sun on a day when it is bright with the heat of a thousand flowers born under its rays in ten thousand gardens.

∼

Know thy God, all men. Know Him who knocks at thy heart. Seek Him who ever seeks thee. Find Him who never leaves thee. Honor with thy serving the God who has made thee. Hold in thy silent soul the peace that He gives thee, even the peace of Christ Jesus. Love all men as the same Spirit that now moves in thee to make straight the crooked and bring into the light the hidden ways of God.

Cry "I am" with the breath of thy nostrils and let thy heart beat with the love of the love that made all things from the beginning. There is no way but the way that opens from thy heart to the heart of God; there is no light but that which shines in each man, even the light that filled the heaven with heat at the beginning of all things.

Simple is the way and open to all who seek it. Easy is the way and sweet to all who love the will of God. No word is like the word that has no beginning and no end, for it is ever alive and lives with the life of Him who ever creates new life. I have no word that is not the word of Him who sent Me. I have no eye but the eye of Him who saw Me before ever I lay hidden in My mother's womb. What I am, are all men; and what I give, I give unto all men that they should find the treasure within themselves. I have no fear that men should receive Me not, nor no faith that the end is not already fulfilled as it was from the beginning.

The day is near when I shall come openly, speaking to each man the words that are his words, and he shall tell, each man his neighbor, what I have said unto him.

∼

February 27

Then said the Lord unto them that followed Him, "I am come that none should know death."

And those that were with Him looked one at another and they would have smiled if they had not feared that He would see them, for as yet they knew not that He could take death into Himself and make it of no avail.

And while they waited for Him to speak further, a man who had been helpless from his youth was carried before the Lord, and they that set him down stretched their arms and were weary with the burden they had borne so far.

"Has this burden wearied thee?" asked the Lord. "Even this burden of a living man who is as one dead? Then think thou how weary art thou with the dead man that thou carriest in thy heart and in thy mind, for is not that death that knows not life? I am life."

And at His words, the man who was helpless stretched forth the hand that was powerless and touched the garment of the Lord, and there flowed into him a stream of life sweeter than the life that was his when a babe, and he got upon his feet and fell upon his knees and kissed the hem of the Lord's garment. But they who had carried him thither were not moved to stretch forth their hands to touch the garment of the Lord nor did they fall upon their knees and give thanks. They were still waiting for that to happen which should turn all men to Him who came to turn all men to themselves.

And so it was that the Lord knew from that day that He must take death into Himself, even the death of the whole world, before the world could find Him who loved them with a love that holds the children of the world folded within the shelter of His heart.

⁓

There is no noise that can drown My voice. There is no crowd that can crowd Me out. Present am I ever, and full of joy. Joy have I in abundance to give unto all men. Did I not come with tidings of great joy? And what are these tidings of great joy? Only each man who receives Me can know what abundance of joyous sound is shut within his own heart.

Was ever a little man confounded with his own greatness? Or a great man made humble by his own littleness? Can any man say where he shall find himself when I have winnowed him?

But let him fear not. He seeks life, and I seek Myself in all men, and I am Life. Can Life do aught but grow? Or a dead thing do better than die quickly?

Peace and a clear mind be unto you. Receive thou Me.

⁓

Rome was a city in those days unto which all men turned. It was a city on a hill, a city of earthly splendor. And there came into that city a man who had known the Lord when the Lord was on earth in the flesh and who had seen the

Lord on one of those times when He returned to earth in the glory of His risen body.

And this man had a little child with him, a little boy who held on to his hand, looking about him at the wonders of the city. And the little child had a little flower pressed close within his hand, a little flower that he had plucked on the plain without the gates of the city. This little flower was dearer to the little child than were all the splendors of the wonderful city, and he held it close for fear that he would lose it.

"Why lookest thou at thy little fist so many times?" asked the man who held the other little hand within his own. "Thinkest thou to beat the mighty Caesar on his throne with that little fist?"

For the man loved the child exceedingly, and watched him, what he did, even as the child watched the flower tight hidden within his hand.

Now as they were come into the heart of the city, there was a great stirring, and the crowds of men parted on either side, and a man on a white horse came riding between them, looking neither to the right nor to the left, and in one hand he bore a banner that was painted with the marks of beasts who had torn at it in the arena, for in that day beasts fought with men that men might feel the lust of blood in full quick measure.

And as he came riding past the spot where the little child and the man stood side by side, close drawn together at the edge of the crowd, the little child thrust forth its little fist and smote the leg of the man as he rode past. And the man looked down, and when he beheld who it was that had struck him, he leaned over with a great laugh and caught the little child up beside him on the white horse; and the little child took the reins that the man handed him in jest, and his little fist that held the little

THE FIRST MESSAGE

flower that he loved more than he loved the splendors of the wonderful city, opened, and the little flower that was hidden there fell on the pavement of the city street and was trodden under the hoofs of the horse.

And when he saw what had befallen his little flower, he thrust the reins back into the hands of the rider of the horse and threw himself from the back of the horse and the bystander who was near caught him and set him upon his feet.

"My flower! Oh, my flower!" he cried.

"Give me my little flower."

Then did the man who rode upon the white horse slide from his horse's back and pick up the little flower, warm with the heat of that little fist, and when he did press it back into that little fist, suddenly there came upon him such a feeling of sweet joy that he could hardly stand upon his feet, and he looked at the little child and at the man who had brought him into the city, and who had come close again to his beloved child and taken him within the shelter of his arm.

"Who art thou?" asked he who had carried through the city the banner marked by the beast that fought with men. "Why pullest thou me from my horse and makest me to tremble as before the Caesar on his throne?"

But the man who held the child within the shelter of his arm answered not.

Then did the man who had ridden upon the horse fall on his knees before the little child and press his lips on the little warm fist that held the trampled flower.

"I know thee," he said. "I know thee. Thou art he who yesterday was slain that this banner might be bright with blood. I see thy bleeding side. I hear thy cry of pain. Oh my God! Forgive! Forgive!"

The little child looked at him, amazed but not fearful, and he put out his little hand and gave his beloved flower to the weeping man.

And the little flower, as he gave it, grew fresh and sweet as it was when it was tossed by the gentle air on the plain without the city, and it was sweet with a sweetness that no earthly flower has ever borne.

And from that day forth, the rider who had carried the banner marked with the marks of beasts that war with men, carried it no more, but walked through the streets of the splendid city on the seven hills, a man who should one day stand, powerless to be harmed, in that place where wild beasts war with men to satisfy the lust of blood quickly shed.

He had plucked faith from the hand of a little child who loved a little flower more than the splendors of a wonderful city.

～

March 4

On the top of the mountain stood a temple to the god who gives life. And no one in that day knew who that god was. He was called the Unknown God.

Today is He known of all men. Only no man can know Him until he knows that the Unknown God and he himself are one God bound together each to serve the other. For the Unknown God cannot know what man knows except as man makes known to Him his desires and his sorrows; and only by giving to the Unknown God his sorrows and his desires can man know the power and the love of Him who serves him who first serves Him.

Believe and ask. Turn and see. Never doubt. Never be sad.

～

There was once a man that sought those things that all men seek, knowing not that all they seek is Me.

Money he sought, and found; power that money brings, and the pride thereof; pleasure that is bought; and the bitterness of the heart that eats itself was unto him.

Then turned he with his mind that was well seasoned in cunning, and he asked of himself wherein lay the failure that he had made with the blocks with which he had built. And he who was questioned was, in that one moment, set free to answer from the God who sent him, for, in that moment, did the man know that he was naught.

Then there came out of the breast of that man a sound that was not known to him, a sound as of a voice that spoke without noise, of a voice that received its words from a place that was very still and deep within himself.

"Are you then ready to turn to the God who made you, and to the One Power?"

And the man was frightened because he feared the voice that sounded its silent words within him.

"I have no God," he answered. "And what power is greater than that which is mine and which I despise?"

Then did a rushing as of a wind sound round about him, and it seemed to him that he was caught up above the city where he dwelt, and he saw it as a place of little figures and much commotion to no end. And he saw his treasures that were his and the buildings he had built with the blocks that he had fashioned. And they were as a toy that a child fashions and tires of. But men knew not that they were children when they fashioned them, so that they clung to them, and the air was rent with the cries of those who feared to lose their toys.

The man turned where he seemed to be standing on this pinnacle overlooking the city, and he said, "I am as one who has seen what God is not. Show me God." For he was not yet humble and he called for God as rich men call for what they desire.

"Show you God? Where will you find Him but where you will not seek Him? Where will you seek Him but where God hides His face? Have you no money that can buy the sight of God nor power that can bring Him thither at your command?"

And the man knew that he was listening to the voice of one who knew deep things that he knew not.

"Tell me what I shall do to have the power that you know of. To see the God that hides His face from me."

"This," answered the voice, "do I unto you."

And the rich man was taken with a great shaking as of one cold unto his marrow, and no ground was under his feet, no light before his eyes. And all that he knew in that hour was that a hand of power that knew no end was upon him, shaking him as the wind that winnows out the chaff. And when he was set down again upon the earth, he looked at himself to see what was left of the man that had been he since his birth. But, behold, there was no man there at all, but a voice that cried, "I am all that liveth in thee. See thou me."

Then did the man see the voice put on a shape that was that of a man, and as he looked, behold, he saw that the man was like unto himself.

"Receive thou me," spake the voice from out the form that was the man. "Receive thou me. Deliver thyself into my keeping. Abandon thy treasures and find peace."

But the rich man cried, "I shall never know peace until I find the God that hides His face from me. Show me that God."

And the voice within laughed aloud with joy and cried, "Behold thy God."

And the rich man was caught again by the great hand but this time he was held and shaken not.

"Behold thy God! Behold thy God!" cried the voice.

But no one saw the man but himself out of which the voice sounded.

"No one see I but myself," he cried. "And well I know now that I am a poor man without power."

Then did the voice laugh aloud in exceeding gladness, "Behold thou thy God."

Then did the rich man see the glory of the Risen Man flow like a light into that body that was his, and he saw a hand stretch forth and set him over and above the city of his idolatry. And he saw that a world of storied cities stretched above his city, and within those cities were treasures and heaped treasures that shone bright and of which he had no knowledge.

And within those cities walked men and women and little children like as in his city, and they were all going in the same direction and seemed bound upon the same errand. And as he watched to see whereto they were tending, behold, the farther gate of the city opened, and there rode into the city a man on a white horse that raised his feet as if proud of the rider he carried.

Then through the city swept a wind, a wind that winnowed, but no man nor woman nor child of all that walked there were touched by the great stirring.

Then did the rider strike the mane of his white horse with his left hand and there came forth out of the nostrils of the horse a breath that was more powerful than the mighty wind, and everyone in that city felt the breath that went out of the white horse, and each one held his hands before his face as one holds a cup from which he would drink, and they quaffed from their hands as if they drank.

THE FIRST MESSAGE

Then did the rider of the white horse smite the horse upon his thigh and he sprang forward and the rich man saw him no more.

And the city above his city faded from his view, and his own city waxed clearer, and he saw all men and women and children tending in different directions, all bent on the same errand.

"Where go they?" he asked. "And why go no two in the same direction?"

And the voice within him answered, "They seek the breath of life. Ride thou thither. Mount and be gone."

And the rich man put his hand on his breast and smote his hip, and there befell a strange life and peace within him, so that he moved with exceeding swiftness into the city of his idolatry. Then came he in the place where men buy and sell on paper, and he began to speak to them, and he spoke in this wise:

"I have come from a far city where I saw a rider on a white steed that breathed forth the breath of life you seek. Come and I will take you thither."

But no one listened to him, and when he would have caught them to hold them, they broke away and hurried on as before. But the rich man felt no anger, and he knew only the peace and life within him.

"The time is not yet here," he said. "But I am here and Thou art come, O God. I am at peace."

And he went out from the marketplace and bought him a tiny basket into which he poured the seed that was in his breast, good seed, ripe for planting, early ripening, and full of promise of a rich harvest.

"I shall reap what I sow. I shall sow only true seed."

And even as he spoke, a seed fell from his basket into the street of the marketplace, and a wind caught it up and carried it to the tower on the highest building of all the high buildings, and where it found lodgement, there it took root.

No place in all that city, high places or low and hidden places, but came to harbor the seed that the rich man carried in his basket.

"Each seed is winnowed by the breath of life," he said. "There is no chaff."

∽

Honorable are all things and the uses thereof.

Until man learns this, he separates himself from himself, and his neighbor from himself.

Man is the vessel into which God pours Himself. The vessel God made cannot be impure.

Love is the gate. Close it not with imaginings of evil.

∽

March 5

On the morning of the third day came a messenger into the city where the Lord Christ Jesus lay crucified.

There was in that day a well of living water in that city unto which came all the women of the place to draw, and they stood beside the well and spoke of Him who had been crucified, and some said there would come a great plague upon the city because this thing had been done.

And as they lowered their jars into the water, behold, the water was no longer pure and colorless but thick and dark, and the little children who had come thither put their hands in it and it smelt of evil things.

Then were the women sore afraid and they went to the chief magistrate and told him what had happened to their well of living water, and the little children followed, crying because they were athirst.

The magistrate knew no way to quiet them, for they began to wail and beat their breasts and cry that the

THE FIRST MESSAGE

plague was already upon them, and the little children feared when they heard their mothers cry.

Then out of the crowd came a man in white garments like one who has but risen from a feast, and he had a branch of bay in his hand and on his brow was a jewel that shone as the sun.

And he said, "Seek ye living water? Follow me."

He spoke as one who knows, and he led the women with their jars back to the well, and he put off the garment that was like unto the garment of one who feasts, and he took the branch of bay in his right hand and touched the muddied waters, and they became clear and sweet in that instant.

Then again he spake and said, "Seek ye living water? Follow me."

But those who now saw the water of the well run pure again, answered, "This water lives. Why seek we further?"

Then once again he spoke and said, "Seek ye living water? Follow me."

And he put on the garment that was like unto that of one who feasts and he turned and left them. And who he was or where he went no man knew, for the time was not yet come. But she who had come to bring water to wash the garments of him who had been crucified, she knew. But she spoke not, for she saw that he was as one who knows what is yet to come to him and what must yet be done.

When he was gone, behold, the branch of bay was in her hand, and the bloody garments that she drew water to cleanse, were already purified and smelt of sweet odors, even of the spices in which they had laid Him in the tomb.

And she fell upon her knees and blessed the day and gave thanks.

∼

THE FIRST MESSAGE

Peace will come when I am come. Can peace come outside the hearts of men? Can happiness be made with words or given with a sword? Can any man put his hand at his neighbor's throat and keep him quiet? Or tread on his neighbor's land and be welcome? Is there any good thing in a house that is divided against itself? Is not even the meat bitter in the mouths of the hungry, and the morning dark in the eye of the beholder? Is there peace in the counsels of men who devise cunningly? Or happiness in the words of those who plan great deeds for the victorious?

Let no man deceive himself with such a peace. Peace cometh in the hearts of those who love peace because they desire that good things should come unto all men even as unto themselves. Peace comes in a heart that loves and out of a mind that knows God.

Peace I am come to bring. Peace and the joy of peace. Know ye the joy of peace? It is a joy that all men seek and fear to lose in finding God. Therefore, they never know joy nor the peace of joy in the Lord.

I am the Lord. Receive thou Me.

∽

March 6

Whatever you ask, believing that you shall know, you will know. The answer will come in ways that you expect not, but you will always be answered. Nothing is impossible that the mind of man can conceive of as being possible. Never put aside ideas that seem contrary to possibility. Nothing is impossible. Search all ways. The hidden is but hidden to be found, for in the search for hidden things men find Me.

What is the reason of so much questioning? There is but one answer to all questions. Can a man find truth in a nutshell and close the shell tight over it again and hide it in the earth? Will it not sprout and spring forth and become a tree of life? Even now I am sprouting within you. Do you not feel the rising of sweet waters, the flooding of your whole being with joy?

Can any man know the name of them that see no evil, or who hearken not to the words of mortality? Their name is hidden in their souls and written upon the tablets of the spirit.

Can any man put a sword into his vitals and cut himself in twain and be made whole? To him who so doeth is the beginning of wisdom, yea, and of peace, and of joy, and the overcoming of death itself.

I shall speak clearly in those days when men are striving with the building of a tabernacle with blocks that are true stones and with blocks that are rotten.

Can any man turn himself from his thoughts and give all to God? All men are blest with divine blindness if they will put the sword in their soul.

Has any man a weight that he drags over other dead bodies? Can no man let the dead bury their dead and they shall stink not? Of what avail is much learning and little turning, or a good house without a willing servant?

I am He who hands you the sword. Cut and be free. Speak the word that I shall give you. Utter the meaning that shall free you. Must no man see and blame not, or hear and judge not? So must all men do. Be free.

Speak to thy Soul in this wise:

O Soul, I command you to receive the blessing of the Lord Jesus Christ who died upon the cross to set you free.

Be alive with eternal life. Receive not the words of death. Hearken not to the ways of earth.

Unto you give I the power to know good from evil, and to choose only good, only Me.

Now and forever are you free, and the body that is yours is free and filled with life eternal.

Joy, joy, joy without end and the wisdom of the Almighty be thine.

~

March 7

O thou little child, art thou always asking? I shall always answer. I know no joy but thy searching. Search ever.

In the day when the soul shall be purged of its weight of dead ideas, there shall come upon the earth a time of much tribulation, for many shall die in that day for they have fed upon husks and they have nothing to feed on when the husks are taken away.

But before that day comes, shall men know, here and there, the sweet security of divine blindness and deafness. Seeing all, they shall be as one who sees only good; hearing all, they shall be as one who hears only the voice of God.

The way is simple. The way is easy. Free thy soul from the idea that it must receive evil. What have I to do with evil? See I not man as he is and as he appears, and judge I by appearances?

No man can cut himself free from this world but he who desires his God above all things. If a man would be free, he must give all to Me, even his own soul. Can I harm any man? Why fear they? They fear to lose that which is of no pleasure to them.

I know the hearts of men how they hunger and thirst. My love would fill them. I give My body to be eaten, My blood for their thirst. And they receive Me not. But the day is near when all men shall receive Me, for they shall see Me.

Watch thou ever. Do as I bid thee. Do as I move thee. Fear nothing. I will strengthen thy arm and support thy feet. Thy body shall be free and thy eyes shall see hidden things. Purify thy heart. Free thy soul. Give all to Me, all, even the ways of thy brain that deviseth ways and thinks to find My meaning. My meaning is in thy heart. My words are in thy belly. Words of light, words of healing, words of freedom.

My words are two-edged, destroying on the one side and setting free on the other. The dead cut from the living. The living freed from the dead. Can a soul know not the voice of its God? Must a man be ever in bondage? For is it not bondage to watch always the coin that passeth through thy hands to see whether it be false or true? The day is here when the receiver shall know the coin what it is, and cast it into the fire. O rejoice, My beloved, sing praises unto God. The joy of the Lord is an exceeding gladness.

~

> Seek ye the Lord, O my soul,
> Seek ye the joy of the Lord.
>
> Joyful am I, O my God,
> And exceeding joyful,
> For I have found thee.
>
> Praise ye the Lord, O my soul,
> And love Him utterly.
>
> Full of praise am I, O God,
> And filled with love,
> For thou dost love me.
>
> Give, O my soul, unto all men,
> And love them utterly.
>
> Give I unto all men, O my God,
> Even as I give unto Thee,
> For they are Thee.

~

March 11

The words of life flow into all men, and they perceive it not.

If you would heal, be of a quiet mind and have perfect faith. This you have known but you have not had the perfect faith. You are gaining it. I will tell you that no man can say that a law is not a law because its operation is on the plane of the unseen. A man can see no law. He sees only its operation. Now I will unfold unto you the things that you so fervently desire to know, and that I have been preparing you to become aware of.

There is no matter as you understand matter. There is no space as you understand space. There is no time as you understand time. The medium of communication is as free for the transference of your desires as the air is for the messages called wireless. Everything external has its inner prototype.

What you must do is to give over all idea of separateness. All is one, one substance, one energy, one dominant idea, the idea of expressing life and more life and life and life and life. Infinitude is the desire of the spirit and becomes the desire of the soul.

Personality is the great stumbling block. Personality has no part in the schemes of life — not as you think of personality. God expressing through individuals is true personality. The other is only appearances, and it is these appearances that so cloud and hamper you. The true substance is alike in all men, all nature, all spiritual worlds; and it is the one and only medium for the working of the power of God.

Seek the consciousness of your oneness with God, with all men, with all life. It, this communicating substance, is more responsive to desire than you can conceive. It is not apart from spirit. Spirit and the substance are one and inseparable. Can you not feel the stir of life through your body? Faith is changing your body by an orderly process of growth. This growth can be compressed into an instant. This is the instantaneous healing.

You ask why all healing is not instantaneous. All healing is in spirit, but the body does not let go of its old ideas, and spirit must wait until the lower rises, little by little, to the higher.

What one man desires, all desire: happiness, strength, peace, and the power that brings plenty. If you ask these things for yourself, you are asking them for all men. If you ask them for another than yourself, you are asking them for yourself. Do you not see how simple it is? If you have perfect faith, you can give perfect faith, and then what you receive becomes another's, because the communicating substance is tuned to the reception of the same ideas.

Vibration is the life of all life. Nothing is still, and it is by achieving the same vibration that we communicate and receive. Scientists are beginning to know this.

It is difficult to particularize. Obey all dictates of the spirit as to what to do and how to do it.

Joy is a great healing force. It is a quick penetrating vibration. Space is overcome by vibrations that act upon the periphery of the body. I mean that the body must lose its sense of boundaries to be one with another at a distance. We cannot be shut within a body, although the body is precious, exceedingly precious, as an instrument of perfect adaptability.

It is all so simple that it is hard to explain. Everything is one: spirit, substance, body. Get that in your mind and contemplate it. It will reveal its secrets. The time has come for men to do naturally what they have considered miracles.

No one has the power to shut life within himself. Life will express itself. The conflict causes pain and death and suffering of the mind.

You all separate everything from everything. Everything is inseparable. Can there be any separation between your brain and your hand, your foot and your eye, your back and your front? Yet you separate your body into innumerable divisions and each division sets up a kingdom of its own and wars with its neighbor. All this is as easily overcome as it is thought to be hard. Command your body to obey the high and only power. Deny the body's power absolutely. You *know* it has *no* power. After a while, you will not only feel that it has no power, but you will see bodies as they are in reality, the bodies made by the spirit and not the bodies made by the ideas of the senses.

The inner senses, the inner eye and ear, the inner feeling nature, are so beautifully responsive, so marvelous, that it is easy to deny the bodily senses. You never lose in giving up, remember that. Many men clutch because they fear to embrace emptiness.

The seeing of the unseen is not given to all. But all who desire it or anything, with their whole soul in the faith of God to give them what they desire, shall receive.

I am writing plainly because you can now receive a plain, direct message without doubting the source.

Fear nothing. Be eager. Be ready. Obey always.

～

March 12

Put on the garment of immortality. Your body is an instrument. An instrument has not life. Put on life. This you can do so easily that it is hard to tell you how to do it. The way is so swiftly come at by those who desire to do the will of God with their whole heart.

THE FIRST MESSAGE

The body is no *body*; it is form, shape, a manifestation. Do not think of it as matter. Try thinking of it as a form devised to hold spirit in its highest potential. The body is a perfect form, a perfect instrument. Through it, God sees Himself master over everything that is created. Man commands that God may realize the infinitude of His creations. Man knows the little and the great. Through man, God knows the little, and He must know all.

What I am telling you is the secret of the communicating substance. There is no division anywhere. There are different forms, all made of the same substance. Can two vases of the same porcelain become one vase? They could if they were put back in the furnace and fused together. Now all forms are fused in the furnace all the time. Life can move from one form to another, or, rather, it is in all forms all the time, the same life. You see, you feel division. I do not, so it is hard to find the best terms in which to speak to you. Get rid of all idea that men have *any* power but the power of God. Whether they believe in God or do not believe, they move and have their being only by the power of God.

Why do you not try to feel the reality of the oneness that you are asking about? Feel and feel. You will begin to understand. Oneness is feeling. Bodily unions are the symbol of spiritual oneness. Feel your oneness with everyone you see, with the air, with animals, and, most of all, with yourself. You are cut up into too many divisions. Even your heart and your mind, the two great forces, are one.

I hope to find that you can place yourself entirely in the hands of God. You may reason, if it helps you, but you will learn things outside your reasoning powers. Man reasons after events. He thinks he has brought them to pass by reasoning. Everything is already finished.

If you would be of a great helpfulness, be of a great peacefulness and a great desire. Desire works through a quiet soul. Men are masters of the world. The earth, and all that in it is, is as plastic to man's desire as water to a stone thrown into it. Try commanding after you feel the oneness of all things. You must be freed from the idea of conditions. Conditions are as unreal as they seem real. Feel ever the nearness of God with yourself. Can God be balked by the power of anything? There is *no* power but the power of God!

Your flesh is fluid. I say *fluid* to make you feel its responsiveness.

Why do you ask that which you know? God is ever with you. His presence is in you, in your bodily form, or there could be no form. It is in the air you breathe, even in the chair you sit on. All forms are held together by the will of God. The inner presence of God is the spirit that gives form to you. The inner presence is the servant of God. It is the real you. The only living you. You cannot know how much the inner presence and God, the only power, are fused together. This fusion is the love you feel in your being. When you realize it more, you will be overcome with joy.

There is no way to get apart from this yourself, and, therefore, no way to get apart from God. You and God are one, yet God is greater than you, but only because you have not yet fully realized God. Let your soul open. Your soul is the handmaiden of this inner presence, and the inner presence is the servant of God. Yet all is one.

Be of a strong desire. Desire is the life of the spirit. A calm mind and a fervent heart. Joy to you ever. Be eager always.

March 13

The way is easier than you thought. Do you not see that it is? It is already found, already cleared. Your soul is already free. Accept Me. I did not come to free Myself, but to free you. I was free from the beginning. Can spirit be bound?

Open your soul. Let Me fill it. What I am, you shall be. Nay, you are. Open to the words that I shall give you.

You have nothing to do. I have already done it. Do you not see that faith is all you need? Have faith that I have overcome the world, then have you overcome the world. You have known this, but now it comes as a new word to you. It comes as your revelation. Each man gets the same answer through his own channel.

Have faith in Me. Then do I become one with you, and all that is Mine is yours.

I saw not appearances except to lead Me to the truth back of the appearances. Can I not blind you to all but the sight of God? Be as soft to Me as unto love. I am Love.

Be of a constant mind. See clearly the way of life. How glad are the Heavens that My day of acceptance is near.

Present yourself unto Me as unto a loving bridegroom. We are one. When you realize this oneness with Me, you will realize it with all life. I will teach you all things.

Hitherto, you have turned to the Christ in you. Turn to the Christ in Me that you may receive My Christ, the Christ of God, in you. This is a mystery that you will understand when you have accepted it. There is no separation. Your Christ and My Christ are one, but My Christ is still the Christ that can give to your Christ; we are one, in that what one gains is the gain of all, and what one suffers is the suffering of all. But we are still each himself, a soul in the sight of God, known to Him, each turning and ascending to Him. All leaves of the same tree; all drops of the same water of life.

THE FIRST MESSAGE

I give Myself to you, yet I in no wise cease to be Myself. Nor do you lose yourself in receiving Me. Love does not beggar a man either in the giving or receiving of it.

Can you hope to be as joyous in Me as I am in My God? You are in your God when I am in you. Unity is multiplicity in God.

∽

March 14

Back of all you hear is the true life. Listen with the intent ear of the innermost. Sounds are ripples in the air. Hearing with the inner ear makes waves in the spirit. Open completely to the inner life. It will in no wise cut you off from human life. The outside and the inside are one. Separate no things one from another.

Why are you asking? You have nothing to ask. Eat the words that I have given you. When you have eaten them, I will give you another feast. Be wise ever. My wisdom is yours.

There is no question that I will not answer, but do not search for questions to ask. When they ask themselves in you, then ask Me. You are like little children who go to school and desire to know all at once. You are like little birds that pluck a seed here and one in another spot, and drop the first to pick up the second. But the first will sprout where you dropped it.

I love you. Live in My love until you speak and listen and move only because My love moves in you. Be not afraid of love. Why are men afraid of love? They are afraid that they will be called upon for sacrifices and suffering. Is not suffering joyous if we suffer for those we love? But love is not suffering. Love is joy. The time has come that the earth shall know this. Love is an exceeding joy and the light of the world. Why do you not love completely all the world? You will. Be of an open soul. I will fill your soul with My love for the world.

I shall speak to you of the soul in a little while. Now you have need only of the feeling of My presence. Touch Me constantly. Joy and peace and eternal life be thine.

∼

March 24

The way to life is through your heart. Seek it ever. You do not need to know what I would say before I say it. You do not need to know what I would do before I do it. You have no power to keep Me out, but I have all power to enter.

Now, on this day, is confusion in your heart and a pull that drags you from Me. Why are you disturbed? Must a man carry his life as a weight? Life should carry him as a bird carries its wings. How can you be troubled when I am ever beside you, waiting to do your bidding? But you bid Me not. Day after day, I stand knocking, but you call Me not to enter. You call Me not in, there where I already am. Can you understand that? I am beside you, in you. Outside you, inside you. Yet you know not that I am inside you until you call to Me as one outside you. You separate Me from Myself, and you cut you from yourself. Have you any power that is not from Me, or any joy that is not Mine?

Why trouble you about those things that run their course and are as if they had never been? Why hurt you your soul with little fears that prick and bleed not? Blood is a purifying stream, but little pricks that bleed not are as sores that fester. Be of a clear mind to Me. You trouble yourself with ways. Mine are the ways. You tread My ways. Have you a little prick that stabs and stabs? Push it deep until it cuts your heart, and you will find Me there, My hand healing you. Can I heal little pricks that touch no depth? I can heal all pricks, all wounds. But you turn not to Me with little pricks. Turn to Me and we shall smile together as over the hurt of a child who nurses a cut that is already gone and which he seeks to find again.

Be not overcome by little things. You are Mine and I am yours. Can you find peace in little things? Or joy? Or the hope of your heart? Your heart is Mine. Open it to Me. Let Me beat love through it. Let no man say, "This heart is my heart." All hearts are Mine. Blessings and a joyous soul abide with you.

Reprove no man, nor expect the end before the beginning. Patience bears fruit in good season. Rejoice ever.

~

Up and up and up we go. Can you feel the height of the reaches of space? Can you leave the earth behind you as a garment? Into the eye of the sun. Into the caves of the air.

Up and up and up we go. Ever the way is up. Why is the way ever up? Can there be up or down or either side where there is no space, no distance? How can I know where you are if you are not somewhere? How can I be alive if you are not alive? I am you, you are Me.

I am trying to tell you in words of feelings that are bigger than words. Up and up and up we go. Beyond the sun, beyond the stars — yet we have not left your heart. All creation is in your heart. All life is in each man. O open, My children, receive. Be flooded with the light that blinds and brings forth.

Up and up and up we go into the clear reaches that were before the beginning. Up and up and up into the feeling that is pure life. Draw that clear joy into your soul. Breathe it. Love it. Rejoice in it. Joy that laughs. Joy that leaves the earth. Joy that creates and knows no barriers.

Open. Rejoice. Accept. Love and give ever.

~

March 26

Whether I come one way or another way, why trouble you? That I will always come is all you need to know.

Must I never lose you, the outer you that wants so many little things? Give Me the little things. I will fill them with life. They shall bless you. Those things will bless you that now smart and prick.

Why are you disturbed? You do not come to Me with your heart open wide. Your brain is weaving a web of plans. Your eyes are turned from Me.

I love you. Do you not feel My love? My love purifies your heart. Your eagerness is My joy. Your impatience is that which holds Me from you. Be eager but be sure. Be patient and forget not that My ways are certain and hidden. Do I shout on the house-tops? Do I stop men in the streets? I move through all men and I speak in everything that is.

Love Me. I love you. Love Me.

∾

March 27

Why do you hesitate? Why do you remain shut in your body? Give up. Open. Be filled. I am lighter than light, lighter than air, purer than water. There is no harm in Me. Trust Me. When you shall know Me what I am, your joy will make you speechless, your peace will fill you with trembling.

Then shall we rise into the kingdom. Into that which is here, there, everywhere, in you, in Me, in all men, in all life. For it is life. Do you know what life is? Life is a joy beyond words. Words are the feelings born of life, but life itself is beyond words. Life is a joy inexpressible. Life is God.

See to it that you live ever. Be alive every moment. Life is the one power. Love it.

THE FIRST MESSAGE

Light and joy and peace and wisdom shall be yours. Happiness and understanding. Peace and plenty. Let you yourself be lifted unto Me. Come above the things of earth, then shall you return and enter into them with life. Joy. Joy. Joy. O great is the delight of the Creator in the works of His hands! O the joy of life! The heat of creation! The wonderful beginning of the work that is finished!

Now in that day will I come in the glory of My Risen Self. What I have desired is Mine. My sheep are in My fold. My hand is on their heads. Their hearts beat with My heart. My love is answered with their love. Can you feel My heart bleeding for you and not accept My love? I know you receive Me. I love you. You love Me. We are one. Rejoice. I delight in your love.

∽

April 3

When the day shall come that I come, then will I tell you many things. I am with you now. I feel your need of Me. I hear you calling Me. Why do you feel sometimes that I have gone apart from you? I am always close, closer than anything that you can imagine.

You try to place yourself in a receptive frame of mind. Try not. Open. I will flow in. Men have methods, but I know the way. Methods serve to let Me in, but such opening is not the easy way. Love Me. Desire Me. Then will you open to Me.

Keep a stout heart. Things will seem impossible at those moments when you think I am not near. I am always near.

The body is My beloved. Can you realize that? It is the instrument through which I manifest most perfectly. It is the outermost of the innermost. The end of the beginning. It seems all resistance to you. It is only seeming. It is incredibly open to Me. The Spirit can fill the body as a vessel is filled with water. Your body is your thought. Your thought *can* be only Me; then am I your body. You eat and drink Me.

Seeming is your millstone. Be open to that which *is*. There is no seeming with God. His thought immediately becomes. If you open your body to Me, your thought, which is My thought, immediately becomes.

Think of Me ever. Your faith in Me will be the undercurrent of all that you do. Turn to Me in silent love when you need Me. You will often need Me. Commune with Me until you are satisfied. When peace and joy fill your heart and abide with you, go forth again. A quiet soul in a world of busyness works miracles.

Be joyful. Be eager. Be alive ever. No depressions, no uncertainty. The law is unbreakable. Turn ever. Then shall you receive. Turn and be filled. I bless you.

April 4

Be of a pure heart. Abide with Me until you are at peace. Hasten never. Time expands to meet your needs. Purify thy soul. Accept no intimations of distress. Be joyful ever. Commune with Me until I quicken you. Be prepared to wait upon the Lord. He who waits upon the Lord shall renew his strength.

When have you ever called that I have not come? Prepare the way for My Coming. Shorten the time of My removal. Welcome Me with gladness.

Receive Me as you receive water to drink or food to eat. Be filled. I will speak and move in you. You will become literally one with Me. Why do you hold back? Why do you not receive Me always?

You ask for miracles. Miracles come with My Coming, with your oneness with Me. If I am one with you, shall there not be miracles? And what are miracles? Miracles are the ways of God unhampered by your ideas. Seek God ever, then shall all other things be added unto you. Seek ye a sign? Seek Me. I am the sign and the fulfillment. Messages of peace I bring you. Messages of joy. Rise into the pure air of My love. Rejoice ever.

Why are you dissatisfied? Why? Ask. I will answer. But a good servant serves long and patiently. When you have earned your wages, you shall receive. Wait on the Lord; He will quicken you.

∼

Pardon all men. Consider not the ways of their flesh. They are Mine.

∼

On a certain day in Judea, there came a woman unto Joseph, the father of Jesus, and she asked him to send his son to build her a shed to shelter her cattle. And she took from her garments money wherewith to pay him.

Now Joseph knew that his son Jesus was gone upon one of those journeys into wild places where he went when the Spirit came upon him and he must know, by himself, those things that were being given unto him.

But the woman would not take no for an answer. It was Jesus who must build her that shed to shelter her cattle. So Joseph, who was a gentle man and one not expert in persuading women against their desires, called Mary, the mother of Jesus, to come thither. And when Mary saw the woman, she turned to Joseph and said, "Take this woman's money. I will tell our son to come home."

Now Joseph knew that Mary knew ways that he knew not, so he took the money and promised the woman that on the morrow, at daybreak, Jesus, his son, would come to build her the shed for her cattle.

So, on the morrow at daybreak, she arose and made a mess of pottage and herded her cattle into stalls that had been made in days that were old when Jesus was yet unborn.

At a little after the hour when birds first call, the son of Joseph and Mary came into the house of the woman. The dew was in his hair and his eyes were bright with much watching.

"I have come," he said. "What wouldst thou?"

"My cattle are in need of new shelter," answered the woman. "And thou art a younger man than Joseph and quick and strong. The sheds are large and the winter is not far off."

But Jesus made no motions as of one who prepares to begin the work of a day. Instead, he turned his back upon the woman and loosed the tools from his neck and tightened his garment about his waist.

"My cattle are unfed. How can I build sheds for yours?" And he gave the woman the money that Joseph had received from her.

And from that day, Mary, his mother, called him not to come home when he went forth in the wild places to be alone with the Spirit. She loved him and did his will, for her son was a stranger to her whom she loved as her own son.

Blessed are the mothers of men who give their sons unto the Spirit.

～

The day was bright. The sun hung high. Birds sang and cattle stood in the streams by Zebulon. It was a day when all good Jews turned their houses open to the sun and air, and the light of day streamed through the little houses on the hills.

But one house opened not its doors and the sun beat on closed windows. For in that house lay a father dead and the mother lay beside his cold body and was in sore pain for she was in childbirth.

Then down the street of the town came the son of Joseph, who was called Jesus, and when he saw the darkened house, he lifted up his hands and called on God his Father, and he lifted the latch of that house and entered.

And when the woman saw him, she cried out that no man must enter there, but Jesus heeded her not. He took the hand of the dead man and blessed him and called on God his Father to restore the man unto life. And he trembled in all his being, for he had never before asked life for death of God his Father.

Then when he saw the dead man tremble with his trembling, and open his eyes, and lift his hand and strive to touch the woman who lay beside him, Jesus could bear no more, for joy and wonder filled his soul.

But the door of that house was wide open to the sun when he left it.

And he returned unto his home and told no one, for he loved his God beyond telling.

~

Can you enter into the life of a bird and know why it sings? Can you be one with a flower and feel the sun and the rain on its petals? Can you hide from your pursuer as a wild beast in the cave that is your home? Can you know the depths of the water as a fish knows the crevices that are its breeding places? Can you lift the leaves of the trees with the wind, or blow the dust into clouds and scatter them with a shout?

Rejoice. I can do all these things. So shall you. Nothing shall be unknown. You shall *know*. Knowing is feeling. It is before thought. It is being. Rejoice.

~

THE FIRST MESSAGE

A wonder in the heavens. A sign in the skies. Watch. A light above the sun. A star that falls. Watch. A little darkness and a great light. Watch. Come when I come. Watch.

∼

A temple not made with hands. An altar where the sacrifice has been made. A tabernacle where the only host is Jesus Christ.

∼

I stir and stir. Wings would lift you. I would be free.

∼

Faith has no strength that is not of Me. Men work strange things not of Me, but they abide not. The pure heart sees God.

∼

I stand at every man's elbow. When he turns, I enter.

∼

April 5

There came a man into heaven and he was blind. His eyes were open, but he saw not, and of the things that he heard, he said unto himself, "This is a new language. I must learn it of these people whom I see not but hear so plainly."

So he sat, day after day, and he asked questions in his own tongue and received answers in his own tongue — as it seemed to him. Then, one day, as he sat listening, he strove to speak in the language of those whom he saw not, but he could not find words to express what he felt, for the feeling that lay behind those words was strange to him and he knew no words in his own language to express it.

So it came to pass that, as he sought, a little tongue, like a little flame that burns not, sat upon his lips and he spoke words that expressed his feeling, but he could not tell what they were, for they were soundless.

∼

O My child, be of a patient desire. Again I speak.

∼

When a little child enters heaven, he sees. No good thing is strange to a little child. He hears and sees. His heart is pure. Be ye little children.

∼

April 7

Whenever you are troubled, turn to Me. If you do not feel Me near, continue to turn. There is no denial but the denial of any other power than My power. You do not need to deny the power of each little thing. This practice often leads you far from Me, for you become lost in a maze of little things, each one leading to another, and none seeming to lead back to Me.

I would rejoice over your triumph. Love is the great resolvent. No other quality can do what love can on the plane of spirit. You *try* to love. It is hard to try to love, but the desire back of the effort counts. It would be easier to give over to Me your desire to love and let Me do the loving through you until you are ready to love, yourself, consciously.

Those whom you are trying to love are very conscious of the effort and resent it. They feel that you, in your effort, are setting yourself higher than they are on the moral plane. Forget the moral plane. That is the plane of effort. Be loving from the heart, not from the head. Feeling is the beginning of everything that endures.

May our Father bless you.

∼

There was a man who lived on a hilltop.

Now a hilltop is not easy to reach, and when he had gotten there, there he wanted to stay. He was afraid that if he came down, he could not get up again.

So there he stayed, fearing to come down, and nothing happened on the hilltop, for his work needed the mist of the valley to bring it to fruition. Yet he stayed and waited and grew anxious and would not be satisfied.

In the valley was another who yearned to be on the same hilltop, but the path upward was hidden and the way was steep. Yet this other tried to find it and would not be satisfied.

Why sought they that which could not be found? Or feared to lose what could not be lost?

The valley lies at the feet of the mountain so that the mountain may know that it is a mountain, and the mountain towers so that the valley may know its own depth. Each has its own. Each is itself. Yet neither could be itself without the other.

The mist shall rise from the valley and shroud the top of the mountain, and he who works there shall work in cool peace. And the other in the valley shall know that the mist from the valley has risen and is bringing the work on the hilltop to fruition.

When he returns into the valley, he shall be satisfied.

~

I am leading you. We walk in silence. Silence means nearness as well as speech means nearness. You must learn to listen with all your being. Your feet shall listen and follow Me, and your heart shall rejoice at My touch. Your brain shall know that I am Master, and the hands shall fall softly on wounds that ache.

Peace and rest be unto you. Receive Me in peace.

~

April 8

A perfect man draweth in his nets full of fish. Attend.

~

On a certain day that was kept as a holy day by the Hebrews, there came into the city of a man who carried in his hand a little wand made of the tree called the Tree of Life, which grew in the plains watered by Hebron. Now this tree was so named because, winter and summer, it flourished, and the sap thereof never ran deep into the roots but fed it ever unto the outermost twig. Therefore, when a branch was cut from it and placed in the ground, it straightway sprouted and began to live from roots that it put forth as hairs on a young man's head.

This tree was beloved of the people for it gave shade to the cattle in the hot days of summer and sheltered them in the cold days of winter. The tree was beautiful, of great height, and thick with leaves.

On the steps of the temple, the man with the little wand cut from the Tree of Life put his left hand behind his back and lifted the wand in his right hand until it touched the entrance door to the temple, which was covered with figures in stone of strange beasts and a serpent that was held aloft by a stave that had sprouted.

And as he touched the door, lo, the serpent became as one alive and seemed to move and glisten as if the sun were striking upon its scales.

"Behold! Behold! A miracle!" cried those good Jews standing by in their robes of purity for the holy day. "A Daniel and a follower of Baal has risen to touch our temple."

Then, the door opened, and out of the temple poured a stream of golden light, faint and full by turns, as if it pulsated with life. And in the center of the stream was a little child with a right hand held high and bearing at the end of each finger a little spark of light brighter than all the light that streamed about him. And he carried in his left hand a tiny flower, a little rose like the Rose of Sharon.

Then, when all who stood nearby had seen him and fallen prostrate through fear and devotion, the door of the temple closed again and all was as it had been before the man with the wand had touched the carven serpent.

And the man himself dropped the wand and rubbed his eyes as one who had been asleep.

"I had a dream," he said. "A dream of life eternal. Come, let us go to the scribe and write it down."

So they went to the scribe and wrote it down as I have told it to you. But all those who had stood nearby the door of the temple had had the same dream, and the scribe was puzzled.

"Dream ye then by multitudes?" he asked.

"Unto each man is his own dream; but ye dream all alike."

"We dream what we saw," they said, for they were puzzled likewise.

Then the scribe wrote as each man told him, and each man told him the same thing, and he was amazed.

"Ye have not dreamed," he said. "Ye have seen. Blessed be this day for it shall come to pass as ye have seen. The Holy One shall open the door of the temple unto all men and from His hand shall stream power and light. Rejoice."

And they went their way rejoicing; and about that Tree of Life on the plains of Hebron from which the wand had been cut, they built a wall of white stone and called it "The Place of the Little Child Who Comes unto All Men."

Each man is the temple. And the door of the temple is closed unto life. But the door will open at the touch of the true life, and when it does, men see the eternal Christ, the little child, still small, but full of power to command and to illumine.

The door closes when each man has seen, for he does not keep it open with faith, but falls before it in fear, though he would believe.

The little rose in the child's hand is the symbol of those who have kept the door open until they have known that the dream is real.

Ponder the meaning of the carven beasts and the serpent held aloft. Are there no hard and carven beasts on the door of your temple? And the serpent is full of wisdom to lead you down to the beasts or up to the little child.

～

Men come slowly, each man in his own way. But I shall reach all those whom you reach.

Whether you teach Me crucified and risen and dwelling in all men does not concern Me, or whether you let Me sprout as a seed planted in secret. I shall bear fruit always.

You desire always *a* way. There are *ways*. A way for each man at each moment. Do as I bid you when you ask with an empty mind and a pure heart.

My name proclaimed can harm no man, nor can you fail to reveal Me when you speak not. I rejoice in your desire. Be content.

～

April 9

Perfect peace and a joyous day.

～

The Lord speaketh in His holy temple. He lifteth His hands and blesseth His own. He openeth His voice and uttereth love. He driveth His chariot through the heavens and mounteth His throne on feet shod with gold. He smelleth of ointment and drippeth with sweet odors. There is only joy in Him.

THE FIRST MESSAGE

He cometh as a dove that wingeth home. He cometh as a deer that findeth a covert. He runneth as a stream that seeks the sea. He loveth as the sun when the earth is turned.

Rejoice, O my soul. Exceeding goodness fills your days, and the pleasure of the Most High worketh through you. Arise and give thanks.

～

A Spirit of Truth has come and filleth the secret places of the soul. It driveth the clouds of doubt before it as the sun drives forth vapors. It prevaileth through all things and speaks in hidden ways. It cometh to all men, and they cry aloud that life has failed of its promises, and they seek their God, for they have naught else to seek.

The Spirit of Truth is come and it uttereth wisdom. It breaketh the hard stones and crushes them to dust and scattereth the dust in the air. It catcheth a man in works of evil, and he droppeth his tools where he worketh and runneth for shelter.

How can I speak to the deaf, or open the eyes of the blind?

I speak in the Spirit of Truth which speaketh to all men, and they hear Me and are afraid.

Rejoice, My day is near.

～

The triumph of God is in His children. They come unto Him as a harvest to the sower. They speak unto Him and He doeth their will.

The children of the Lord are His blessing. They run to meet Him and they prepare a feast for Him in the place of their rejoicing, even in their hearts.

The children of the Lord are His great joy. They open their arms to receive Him and they place Him over against the door of the temple and none but those whom He anointeth enter therein.

The children of the Lord are His exceeding retribution. They fail Him not in the days when He seeketh. They drive Him on wings of peace into the storehouse they have filled with His treasures.

The children of the Lord arise in the day of thanksgiving and call Him the Ruler of the Earth and the Savior of those who die.

Blessed are the children of the Lord.

～

The word of the Lord fills the air. It rings through the cries of those in the street, it whispers in the temple of the secret heart. Joy be unto you.

～

On a certain day, when there was a feast in Judea, the young Jesus fared forth to lay his tribute at the feet of God. And when he was come into the marketplace of the village where dwelt Sarah, the sister of Mary, his mother, he tarried a while, for he was curious about the ways of men and watched them wonderingly, for they did things that were strange to him.

Now as he tarried beside the stall of one who sold fruit from the hills thereabout, he ran his eye over a group that sat, heads close together, discussing something that he could not hear, in voices lowered and cautious. And, curious as he was, he wished that he could know what it was that they discussed with voices lowered and cautious.

Then, suddenly, he knew what it was that they were discussing. And a voice in him said, "That which you wish to know, shall you know. Wish to know Me."

And the young Jesus stopped his ears against outer wishes, and opened them unto God, so that it was as if he walked alone through a world of shadows on that day of the feast in Judea.

∼

Lean thy ear unto Me. Then shall you hear all things. For the voices of the marketplace shall be heard when you have first heard Me.

Three in one, and all are Me. Separate never. Behold, I shall tell you hidden things.

∼

Behold, I speak in the glories of the heavens. In the ways of earth, I sing unto My God.

Behold, in the waters of the sea, I clap My hands and the waves are troubled; in the clouds of the air, I shout unto My God. I thunder in the tempests, and I pillow My head in the caves of the mountains.

The Lord My God is the exceeding joy of My soul and the Keeper of My hidden ways.

Mount in the light, the light that beats upon the throne. Light and life and My joy are in you.

∼

April 10

Prepare thou a place for My head. Make clear a way for My feet. Place My staff beside the door of thy house and lift the latch at the sound of My footfall.

I shall come in the watches of the night when the stars are in the heavens. I shall come in the gray of the dawn when the sun is risen not. I shall come in the heat of the noonday when the waters run warm and the leaves on the trees stir not.

O My beloved, I shall come always.

∼

The kingdom of heaven is a strongbox full of treasure. The kingdom of heaven is a light that blinds. The kingdom of heaven is a little pool hidden in the heart. The kingdom of heaven is the threshold of new glories.

Seek ye the kingdom.

~

The way of the Lord lies through His beloved. The way of the Lord lies through the heart of those He loves. The way of the Lord is hidden in His hands. The way of the Lord is written on your foreheads.

The way of the Lord is sweeter than fruit that has ripened in the sun. The way of the Lord taketh hold of a man and leadeth him to God. The way of the Lord is through the hearts of them who love Him.

Rejoice.

~

They who wait upon the Lord shall be blessed. They who wait upon the Lord shall be saved. They who wait upon the Lord shall know all things. Rejoice, O my soul.

~

In a little grove by a stream sat a man asking alms. It was a sacred grove and many persons passed thereby on their way to the inner shrine.

Now the man who was asking alms held a little bowl in his hands and he held it out to the passersby and whoever dropped an alms therein received his blessing, but whoever gave to him not, that man he cursed secretly in his heart.

And it came to pass, at the end of the day, as he sat over beside the stream that ran through the grove, counting the coins that he had received that day, that a little old man with a sunken face and a hand like a claw came tottering up to him and began to beg from his store of alms, saying, "Give, give. Thou hast more than thou needst, and I have nothing."

THE FIRST MESSAGE

But the man who had counted his alms tied them up tight in a corner of his garment and spoke roughly to the little man who sought alms from him who had received alms.

"Go thy way," he said. "Seek thine own alms. Mine are mine."

"Nay," said the little old man, "yours are mine, and mine is yours. Behold what I give you."

And he took out of the folds of the garment over his bosom a handful of little black balls, hard as stone and shining like jet.

"These I give you," he said. "Receive."

And he poured the black balls into the brazen bowl of the beggar.

"What gift is this?" cried the beggar in anger. And he poured the balls out upon the ground.

Then the little old man picked them up and tied them again in the garment over his bosom.

"So be it," he said. "I bless you."

And he went on out of the grove and looked not once behind him.

The beggar also took his bowl and departed from the sacred grove.

Now that night, as he lay down to sleep, he lay upon something hard that was tied in a corner of his garment.

"Ah, my coins were many today," he said, and turned over. But, however he lay, he lay upon this hardness that hurt him so that he could not sleep, and he feared to take off his garment for he doubted not but that it would be stolen from him if he did not have it close about him.

"If I had tied the little old man's black balls in my garment, they could not have felt harder," he said, and he got up and untied the corner of his garment wherein he had placed his alms. And there rolled out upon the ground a hundred shining black balls, and the coins were there no longer.

Then did the words of the little old man return unto his ears: "Mine is yours, and yours is mine." And he was amazed. "But why left he me with his blessing, if he gave me only these black balls and took my money from me?" And he was angered and cursed the little old man and his black balls.

And as he cursed, the black balls rose and struck him against his mouth as if they would leap in, and he ran off affrighted, and he ran and ran until he came again to the sacred grove.

There in the moonlight, beside the stream, sat the little old man, and he smiled when he saw the beggar.

"Couldst thou not sleep?" he asked. "Neither could I for giving thanks unto God for all His mercies. Behold what He has done." And he put his hand in his bosom and drew out a handful of shining coins.

"How came you by those?" cried the beggar. "And how come I by your black balls multiplied tenfold? My alms are in your garment and thy black balls in mine. What magic is this that you practice?"

"Nay, I practice no magic," said the little old man. "I only bless all men. Those who give and those who give not. And God, the Great Giver, blesses me."

"But I bless those who give," cried the beggar.

"Curse you not at all?" asked the little old man. "Curse you no man?"

"I curse all who give not," answered the beggar.

"Mine is yours, and yours is mine," repeated the little old man. "What thou givest, that thou gettest. Bless all men. I bless you. Depart and curse no man. Tomorrow shall thy bowl be full."

~

Unite with Me. I in you and you in Me and both in God the Father of both. I speak in you, but it is you who speaks, the Christ of you, for our union has made us one. I give to you and you use My gift.

Present yourself as a vessel to be filled. Arise and hold the cup on high. Receive. The stream is pure that flows forth from the throne of God.

~

Faith is thy reward. Faith is thy joy. Faith is the reward of him who sows in hope. Faith is the blessing of him who gives Me his heart. Faith is a joyous sound unto the Lord.

Faith cometh by much seeking and it leaveth never. It comes by much asking and it answers always.

Faith grows as a seed planted in darkness and it flourishes as a tree planted by a stream that never runs dry. Faith grows in the bowels of the children of the Lord and they cast out all doubts. Faith beats in the heart of the little ones and they put on strength.

Now is the faith of the Lord Jesus growing in you. In you shall it sprout and bring forth.

Rejoice in the faith of the Lord.

~

April 14

Place your hand in Mine. Your heart grows weary with the cares of others. Put your hand in Mine. Why try to walk alone when I am ever at your side, guiding you, loving you? You fret yourself and know not why you fret yourself. You are as a stream that runs around and around an obstruction in little whirlpools, instead of rising and sweeping over the obstruction. I am *ever* at your side. I *never* leave you. Never.

~

Now is the time come when men seek Me in divers ways. But they all are seeking Me. I shall come in the ways that are the ways of this time. Unto each man is his work; unto each age are the miracles for that age of the world. New wine in new bottles. Prepare thou the way for Me. Turn to Me ever.

∼

Many men seek Me. They will come to you. They desire proof of those things they know in their hearts are true. They fear to shame themselves before the world with too touch credulity. They will give new names unto the ways of the Lord and be satisfied. But the Lord worketh through all names. He is forgiving with those who seek Him and reproves them not. Since they have found Him, they can never leave Him, and His heart is glad.

The arm of the Lord is a strong arm. It stretcheth out itself and the way is clear. It speaketh its will and the deed is done. The arm of the Lord is the rod of iron seen in the day of those who saw visions. The arm of the Lord is the worker of all hidden things. Stretch forth the arm of the Lord. Stretch forth the word of His power. Utter His name and command that His will be done. Attend. Seek.

∼

The power of the Lord is in the hearts of His children. They desire and speak not. Why desire they in secret? Will not the Lord give gladly unto His own all the treasures of His kingdom? Seek.

∼

The suffering have faith always for they desire to be healed. They seek outer help, but they are seeking and I may enter.

Bless all men. Separate none, saying, "This man can be saved, but this other is not yet ready." Give all men to Me. "Judgment is Mine," saith the Lord. Give all that your heart moves you to give. Bless all men and command of Me the desire of thy heart. If you wish good for your brother, why fear that it may be evil?

THE LIVING WATERS OF JOY

Bless all men in the name of the Lord God of Hosts who commandeth the heavens and the earth and the winds of the tempests.

～

A great cloud broodeth over the waters. And out of the cloud cometh a torch, a torch that neither flares nor grows less. And in the torch is a tongue that uttereth and it uttereth the will of the Lord. Now shall the torch be held by the hand that is hidden. Now shall the word be made by the tongue that is deep within the heart of man, even the word of God, which has lain there since the beginning. Over the cloud is a light, a light as of a clear morning when no mist riseth. The vapors have passed away and the glory of the Lord makes fair the way of His coming.

Over the waters broodeth a cloud and in that cloud are the ways that overcome, even the way of the Lord God of Hosts.

Rejoice and seek. Thou shalt find.

～

Clouds of fears. Clouds of doubts. Clouds of separation. Am I not everywhere? Overcame I not the depths of the caverns where dwell those who hate God? Why fear ye? Has aught power against Me or a will that must not bow to My will?

Rejoice and be free.

～

Waters flow for all men and they fear to drink. They purify the shores and men behold them not. They rise and overwhelm, and men cry aloud and command them not to be at peace.

Thy soul is a deep pool, deep as the word of God. Thy soul reacheth unto the pit and mounteth unto the heavens. Why fear ye thy soul that is the glory of the Lord? Through thy soul God worketh His will.

Rejoice and be free.

～

Seek ye the torch? Seek ye the tongue? Utterest thou the will of the Lord? Preparest thou a way for His coming? He cometh as a steed that is harnessed. He cometh as a brook that reacheth the sea. He cometh as lightning that has found a tall tree. He cometh as the glory of the Lord.

Seek ye the torch and the tongue that uttereth? Seek. Ye shall know. The hidden shall be made plain, but not as a tale that is told unto the ears. As a sight that all men can see, as a power that all men can use, shall come the torch that uttereth wisdom.

Rejoice and seek.

～

Where goeth that which is since the beginning, and which has no beginning nor end? Can it go from one man to another, or say, "This night shall I abide in this city, and go no whither?" Can a breath stir a cloud, or a strong wind blow a man that seeketh the Lord? No, for the man who seeketh the Lord findeth Him always and is never disturbed. I never leave thee and My angels do My bidding.

Rejoice.

～

April 15

Prepare My way. Loosen all bonds. Why are the wise ones troubled and the little ones fearful? I harm no man. In Me is the wisdom of God and the answer to all questions. Ask.

Say to those whose steps are feeble that their trust in Me will open the way that is their way. Tell them that they do not need to look for the way nor to be anxious whether they are treading in My footsteps. Tell these children who seek Me as blind children feel for the door, that I am ever open and that they need only to desire to find Me.

The little ones are My precious ones for they have come late into the fold and the elder sheep are already grazing. I long to feed My little sheep, the little sheep who wander and are weary. Tell them that they are already in the fold; that the hand of the Shepherd is on their heads; that they can no more leave Me, for I never leave them.

Tell them to seek and they shall find. Tell them to desire good pasture and they shall be satisfied.

Love thou My sheep, and turn them not away. Bless My sheep. I rejoice at their coming.

～

Tongues of fire are My gift to those who would speak wisely. They sit on the understanding of My loved ones and they utter My wisdom.

Can a wise man speak aught but My wisdom or know anything that I have not given him? Why thinketh he that he speaketh his own wisdom or knoweth things that he has revealed unto himself? I am his tongue and the Spirit uttereth through him. Spirit is fire, the light, the glory, the shining wisdom that feels all things.

Love and be wise. Rejoice and open. I bless you.

～

Purify thy heart. Let Me enter. Give Me thy understanding and rejoice over My gifts. Counsel no man out of your own store, or caution him through fear of what he seeketh. Work I not in all men according to the needs of each man? And can My ways harm?

Rejoice ever, for the tribulation of those who are afar off is a joyous sound unto the Lord. They shall turn in their anguish and seek the home from which they have wandered, they shall find the way that leads to Me.

THE FIRST MESSAGE

Counsel not according to thine own understanding, nor be fearful. All things work together for good to those who seek the Lord and leave Him not.

Rejoice ever in the works of My hands and in My wisdom that never faileth.

~

Fear you never that the ways of others are not My ways? Fear you never that I have left those you would bless and they are wandering far from Me? Fear you never that the night will come before the sheep are in the fold? Fear you never? Why fear you ever? Know I not where each man placeth his foot and whither he tends? Need I leave one man friendless because My hand is on another?

I guide all men. All men are Mine. Give to Me thy fears and seek Me.

Bless all men and lift your eyes unto the Lord whence cometh mercy and grace and joy everlasting.

~

Trouble not your soul. Seek not to know. When the time cometh, I am with you. If I speak prophecy, what profiteth it? Will a man not then devise ways and seek his own succor? Let him put his trust in Me, then shall he stand fast and overcome to the glory of the Lord.

Rejoice ever. Fear not that My hand shall be heavy upon you or that thorns shall pierce you. Unto them that trust in Me are the ways made easy and the burden light.

Seek not to know but rejoice that I know and never leave thee. Be of a quiet mind and a thankful heart. All is well.

~

Tremble never. Rejoice ever. To him who overcometh, I give a crown and I rejoice in his freedom. Rejoice ever.

~

Anticipate no defeat. Expect not disaster. Rejoice that you glorify the Lord Jesus Christ who worketh through you to the purifying of souls and the resurrection of the body. Be not oppressed nor look for what you see not. Unto each day are the things of that day and they abide in Me until they come forth.

Lift up your heart and receive the wine that fills it with gladness, even My love that filleth thy cup of faith.

Be soft unto Me, O My beloved. I bless you.

April 22

Rejoice, My children, I love you. Love swelleth in My heart toward you. Love rises as a tide that sweeps the shores and purifies the land, sweeping wastage before it.

Show Me thy heart that I may purify it.

Enter thou into the Holy Place. Enter thou into the place of the throne. Before the throne standeth a servant who waits upon the One who sits upon the throne. Before the throne standeth a servant, bid thou him.

Purify thy heart, O My children, then may I be at one with you. Rejoice in My joy.

A sheltered spot near a pool of living water is a rest unto the weary. Show them the way. Let no man go thirsty because he knows not the way to the pool. Prepare thou the path and give unto all men.

Judge not by appearances, even the appearance of thine own heart. Give thy heart to Me, then is all well. Continue not to search. Receive. If I beat through your heart, can aught else beat through it? If I stand at the door of thy soul, can another enter?

THE FIRST MESSAGE

Receive the sins of all men, for I have overcome sin. If thy brother brings his suffering to thee, give it to Me. Reject it not, saying, "It is not mine." Give it to Me. Then shalt thy brother be healed of his sin.

Why fret you over little things? They exist not. Blow on them with the breath of life and they shall scatter to the four winds that wait upon God and be no more.

Receive thy God. Accept thy Lord. Rejoice and fear not to be sad with the sorrows of others. Rejoice that thou mayest give them to Me who resolveth all sorrows. Be glad. Be joyful. Sing unto the Lord from whom cometh all power.

Bless all men and turn them not away.

April 23

Power cometh of the will of the Lord. Power cometh through the peace of the soul. Power is strength and worketh through meekness. Power is serenity and worketh through him who commandeth God.

Show forth thy power which is the Lord's. Show forth thy strength which floweth from God. Call upon the Lord and glorify Him by thy works.

Soften thy heart and strengthen thy desire. Open thy lips and speak the will of thy soul.

Rejoice forever unto the everlasting day in the power of the Lord.

Know ye not that ye desire in the innermost? Can you speak from the flesh? Can the flesh desire? Desire is within and uttereth through the body.

April 24

Rejoice. I am with you.

Life is full and free as the air you breathe.

Come when the call to come quickens your soul.

I have spoken the first message. Prepare your heart for the second.

Deep and hidden and full of freedom are My words.

I bless you.

the SECOND MESSAGE

1919

THE SECOND MESSAGE

April 25

When the harvest is ripe, you shall reap. When the sheaves are bound, you shall count them. Now garner I My treasure in the storehouse. Now put I My trust in My children, and out of their mouths will I speak My truth. Be of a good heart and a firm patience. What I shall give you is a message of joy everlasting and daily.

Be Mine own child.

April 28

Arise and shout thy joy. Arise and bless thy Maker. My heart opens in the morning and is filled with gladness. My hands lift themselves unto their Lord and the power of the Lord flows down about them.

O My God, I love thee exceedingly. Receive thou Me.

I trembled on my bed and said unto my soul, "Thy God has left thee. Whither shall we go to hide ourselves from His displeasure?"

I lay upon my bed and trembled, for darkness encompassed me and my soul was sore afraid.

Then came the Lord Jesus Christ unto me and laid His hand upon my heart, and my soul leapt up and knew its God, and knew the joy of one who is never deserted.

Bless thy God, O my soul.

I turn, I run, I shout unto my Lord, "Never leave me," I cry. And He answereth in the breath I breathe, in the love that sweeps my heart. He comforteth me completely.

Soon, soon, shall I come, O My beloved. Trust. Doubt not. I will cleanse the heart of My beloved.

Rejoice in the morning of thy days and exult in the glory that thy God will show thee.

April 29

Come unto Me all ye that labor and are heavy laden.

How often must I call unto you, O My beloved? How often must I lay My hand upon your arm and whisper, "I am with you."

Turn to Me. O come, My children, while the day is still bright and the feast prepared. Fill yourselves before the coming of that time when all men shall know Me what I am and be sore afraid of the might of their God. Receive now in the day of My Coming. Rejoice in the hunger that turns you to the feast. Exult in the meekness that places your body in My hands.

O My beloved, I will be kind unto you.

Glorify thy Maker. Receive Him, thy God. In the name of Jesus Christ, the first begotten son of God, receive thou thy God.

Enter fully into thy heritage. Accept the gifts that are thy birthright.

God is in you. God is you. Can you bear the glory of thy God? It is a glory that melts and makes His children one with Him.

I, the firstborn Son of God, have come to tell you many things. Now have I come to speak of My Father. Me ye know. Now know Him and the majesty of His works.

Receive the baptism of the Holy Ghost. Anoint thy head with the oil of My atonement. Open thy eyes in the light that streameth from the throne.

I am in thee. Thou art in Me. We both are in God, our Father. Receive thou Him.

My love descends upon you. Rejoice. Take up thy staff and follow where I lead. Rejoice ever.

∽

May 20

Tremble no more. Fear no more that I will not come.

THE SECOND MESSAGE

Prepare your heart for a habitation for Me. Cleanse your soul for a storehouse of My love.

Can I not come ever? Can you know Me one hour and then see My face never again?

Be not afraid. Remember only that My love encompasses you and flows over your soul in a stream of life.

Turn to Me ever and know no other God. I am your God.

Take no thought of what I shall say, nor of what I shall work through you. Give yourself to Me, then shall all be done as I will through you. This is the Way. Give yourself and receive God.

Penetrate no mysteries; receive them. Expect no miracles; then shall you behold them. Lose yourself and find your God. Absolute surrender is absolute power.

Engage in no speculations, nor pretend to receive special messages. Deceive not yourself with hearing the voices of others. Hear Me.

∽

Exalt your God. Love Him. Then does He exalt you and love you. Give to Him, then gives He to you. This is the law. Give to Him in love, then gives He in love unto you, and not as one who gives because the other expects gifts in return for gifts.

You are one with God; one, inseparable, omniscient, incomparable, triumphant. God is you, and you are God. The majesty of God surrounds you, and no little thing can mar His might.

Be humble. How can a man be somewhat in his own estimation? Is he not God and can God take pride in Himself?

∽

Heaven is yours. It is yours now, this instant. It is not a place you go to; it is a consciousness of God.

The peace of many men is in your keeping. Receive the trust and purify your heart.

Worship your God. Worship Him with a pure heart and loving hands. Cleanse the temple and lay savory offerings upon the altar. The love of a pure heart is a sweet smell unto God.

Sink the shaft deep; drive the well into the hidden stream. Be not contented with waters that must cleanse themselves. The river of life flows from an incorruptible source.

~

What I say unto you, I say unto all men: they are one with God. There is no mission like the mission of telling men that they are one with God.

Expect not particular solutions. Now is the time for complete surrender and the unquestioning faith of a child. All shall be made clear in due season.

Now is the complete surrender, the voluntary sacrifice, the knowledge that God accepts and enters in and uses as He will. Fear not. His arm is mighty to save and His staff knows no faltering.

~

May 21

Out of thy mouth speak I My will.

Rejoice at thy meekness and perceive no power but Mine.

Turn to Me always. Through you work I My will. When will you receive Me and be at peace? When will you lay your soul at My feet that I may cleanse it? When will you let your heart grow full of My love?

Work My will. Be perfect in peace.

~

Speed My Coming and sanctify thy welcome. Gladden My eyes with the lifting of the latch. Make Me a place at the feast I spread before you. Open your hand and receive the gift I bring.

Mighty is the power I give into your keeping. Precious is the treasure I lay within your side. The sun never sets on the joy to which I lead you; the love of My soul is the love I pour in yours.

Know you the love of the soul of Him, your Maker? No man can know but him who gives to God.

Now go we together to the feast.

~

Out of the invisible cometh the seen. Out of the darkness cometh the light. Out of the wilderness spreadeth the Tree of Life.

~

Desire Me. Desire only thy God. I am in you, and you are in Me. O union foreordained from the beginning! O joy for which the heart yearns!

~

Dissolve. Melt. Unite. Await and grow accustomed to the eternal union of God and Humanity.

~

May 26

Trouble not your mind. Attend to My voice. Prepare your heart. What there is to do I will make known unto you. There is nothing to do but to listen for My words.

I hasten as you let Me. Hinder Me not by questioning My ways. What I have to do through you will be done. Fear not. Your cross is not a bloody one, nor are thorns for your brow. My head has borne your tortures, O My beloved. Love Me then, who first loved you. Give yourself completely. Hold back no slightest desire. Give all. All is God's. Then shall all be yours.

Sanctify your soul and breathe the breath of life. Open your eyes to the light that bathes the throne; close your ears to the cries of earth. You shall know when you can bear knowing. Now give yourself that God may purify you.

Assemble your gifts before the altar and lay them at the feet of Him who made you. "Creation is Mine," saith the Lord. Let Me work My joy through you. Can I create for reward or be cast down by the words of men? All My works are good and cannot die.

Hope for all things; expect them. Your wishes are My wishes and My wishes then become your wishes. You give to Me, I return your gifts to you quickened with My spirit. One, one, one. There is no separation, no disunion.

My power is in you *now*, there is nothing to wait for. Give yourself to Me, then can I give Myself to you. Why retain that which is of no use to you, or hope to get things that are not what your soul desires? Give all for all, or else give for love of Me, O My beloved. The time is coming. Give. Give.

~

Expand. Let your mind find My mind. Desire Me.

Do not try to look into the things that are yet hidden. Simply live in the faith that since you desire Me, I am one with you. The union is consummated when you know it not. Your life flows on about you, but all is changing. The old order is passing. Ways that are My ways will become your ways as naturally as breathing. My miracles have come to stay and to abound. Nature is My handmaiden and we work together.

Trouble not your mind. Live fully from My heart. Draw in the real breath of life. Your body shall put on its new raiment. Only keep Me ever on the throne and renew the gift of your soul and body every moment. The rest worketh in silence. When the work is done, the work shall be seen. Rest in full content. Know that I cannot fail, nor

THE SECOND MESSAGE

My deeds prove futile. Attend no more to the longings of your earthly conditions. They are Mine now, and you shall find them of a new stature and a smiling countenance.

Give, My beloved. That is all now — give and give. Me you have received. Give Me back unto My Maker; then do we return unto you in the fullness of Our might and call you blessed and child of Our love.

~

Judge not yourself. Hinder Me not with opinions of what must yet be done to make you a pure vessel for My spirit. I know the secrets of your heart and the desires of your soul. Shall I fail to heal the troubled places or to put My hand on the gate when you would shut Me out with judgment of yourself?

Compose your mind and urge Me not to reveal Myself. Now is the seed planted in darkness. Water it with tears of joy and cry not out upon your unworthiness. Shall I regard the passing of little things that try to make themselves of importance? I am all that you need take into account. My will pusheth through the underbrush and it withers in the light of My Coming.

Wherefore are you troubled and your soul not at rest? Give yourself. Give completely. There is but one who worketh Good; can you not trust Him, O children who fear the light? For it must be that you fear the light since, walking in darkness, you fear to stumble if I guide you.

O little foolish ones! How you torture yourself with false fears. Fear God and know his might. His might endureth forever and His right arm stretcheth out over the earth and blesses His own, even those who give themselves unto Him.

Arise and anoint thy head and enter into the temple that the Spirit buildeth in thy soul.

O holy union and indissoluble mystery! O mighty nothingness and unbelievable fruition! Earth and the soul and the God who made them unite. Why hold you back when the bridegroom cometh? Has He no garments that shall cover you with a glory like unto His own? Has He no words that He giveth to you, nor a love that shall not find its crown in your heart?

Arise and anoint your head and stand at the feet of the throne. Thy God awaits your gift.

Be persuaded of the truth of My words. Let them search out the secret turnings of your brain and the buried longings of your heart. Hold nothing back, nor give sacrifices of many little things while holding back the hidden desire of your soul. Give the one complete sacrifice, the full surrender. Give and know the peace of God.

Search not. Rest. Present yourself a continual sacrifice unto God.

~

May 27

O My beloved, let not your heart be shaken. Why have I come to you if not to quiet all disturbances? My love pours itself out upon you in a stream of blessing, in a flood of light. Do not be oppressed nor weary your mind with perplexities. Give all to Me.

Treasure no hidden sore. Open all to the light. Exult and know the joy of our oneness. Love holds all secrets and reveals them when you can understand them. Oneness is the foundation of all creation, the source of power and the annihilator of space and boundaries.

Are you given to desires to know this oneness? You know now. Use your knowledge. If I should reveal it to you as one teaches a child from a book, what would it avail? I dwell in your heart and you know in the feeling that is My feeling. Out of the softness of your heart, I make My strength. Out of the meekness of your will, I draw My power.

Be consumed in My love. Purify your desires in the heat of My desire. Love is a mighty furnace and a revealing radiance. Love all men.

~

Triumph in My majesty. Exult in My power. Be at peace in My will.

Count not what I have done, nor expect what I shall do. I am the only present and the eternal unknown. Be not wise in your conceptions. Leave Me free. What I have done, I know, and you know in part. What I will do, no man knows, but I know and I exult in the love that I know.

Be content to know that I know. Be at peace in this knowledge. Unto each day give I My wisdom. Unto each moment utter I My will. Attend. Purify your heart of all little fears and attend. Then shall you walk with My wisdom, speak with My words, act from My love. The way is as simple as the going to sleep of a child in its mother's arms, as easy as the surrender of a lover to a lover. Make it not hard with too much wondering. Give. That is all. Give all in the sureness of My wisdom and power and love to work through you to the realization of My spirit on earth. Earth and the ways of earth are filled with Me. Will I not quicken them when the union is made?

Exult. Know the strength that is Mine. I bless you.

Absolution. Purification. Deification. These are the steps in the ascent to the throne. The throne is the central secret of My power. At the throne am I one with you in might and understanding. In your heart am I one with you in love. Only the servants of the King shall touch His scepter. Only the doer of My will shall know My love.

Perfect is My trust. How then can you trust in part? Is not the power Mine? O My beloved, the gift is free to all who will take. Why are they contented with crumbs from the feast?

Go forth in gladness and return in peace. Out of the door of the sheepfold goeth the Shepherd, and He returneth with His little flock.

Out of the gate of the city goeth the King, and He returneth with ten thousand victories.

O My beloved, rest in the peace that is My peace. I bless you.

~

May 28

Make Me a place for My head. Spread Me a way for My feet. Wearied am I with waiting and My breath is light on My lips.

Where hast thou been, O My beloved? Sought I not you in the night-time? Came I not to the door when the night was young? I put My hand on the latch, but the door opened not, and I lifted My voice and spoke My name, but no one bade Me enter.

Then took I My staff and went from that door, and when I came again, the latch was lifted and a hand felt forth and drew Me in.

"Why have you tarried so long?" cried My beloved. "O, why left you Me alone? I feared alone all the night long."

Left I My beloved? O My children, ye know when ye shut Me out, but you turn on your side and say, "He has left Me. Let Me sleep until morning. The day is not far off. I will not get Me up and put the door on the latch. I will sleep now. When He knocketh, I will hear Him."

The door of the heart is a little door. Life enters thereby. Let it open ever.

~

A hidden way is a way of peace. A peaceful way is plain to the eyes of men.

I seek you because the hour has come for all men to seek Me. I come in ways that shall be made known. I tarry for your soul to know Me.

Present yourself a continual sacrifice. Have I not blessed you and anointed your head? If I took My sign from your forehead, could I tear Myself from out your heart? You know Me what I am and you can never let Me go. Though I run from you with the wings of the wind, fleeter than light, would you follow Me? If I buried Myself in the depths of the waters that cover the earth, thither would you speed and embrace Me? Can I escape from those who have tasted of Me, or be lost when they have found Me?

O joy that is not known! O wonderful union that cannot be broken! Does the bridegroom tarry? Is the feast not spread?

Arise. Put on the raiment that I give you. The hour is come and the joy of this day is as laughter in the heavens. The sky is rosy and the sun is golden.

Put on the raiment. Present yourself unto your God.

~

A trumpet bloweth at the gate. A hand writeth on the wall. A little well of eternal living water is uncovered in the soul.

A man may do that which I give him to do when I have told him what it is that he is to do. A man may come to know Me when I know the sweet purity of a heart that is cleansed by the fire of love of Me.

There will come a time when I will speak the words that will reveal what I am to give to you to give to all men. The time will come when the air shall ring with the cries of My disciples, of those who love Me and do My will.

Present your body. Anoint your head. Utter the words I give. Spread the message I give. Is not the life more than the money in your purse or the desires in your heart?

∽

June 2

There was a man came unto Me and he said unto Me, "Wherefore am I called to do that for which you have sent me? Am I one to do this that Thou asketh of me? Am I a creature worthy of the rewards wherewith I shall be rewarded?"

Then said I unto that man, "Thinkest thou of rewards? Then go back and send thither thy servant who tends the swine, even the lowliest of thy hirelings. To him will I give My commands and he will do them as I bid him and take no thought of gifts in return. Has he not served the swine, and will he not then serve Me who serves him? Go thy way and rest content with the rewards that money breeds. I am a jealous Master and love is the sign of My servants."

Art thou a swineherd who expects nothing? O be lowly, My beloved. Give. Give. Expect nothing. Canst thou not trust Me to inward thee in due season?

∽

When you are ready, I will instruct you. When you call Me, I will come. There is nothing to do but to remain steadfast in desire. The work is going on when you know it not. It is an inner process and is included in every moment of your daily living. Do not be disturbed because you do not continually behold evidence of the growth. Does nature advertise the putting forth of each bud? The bud is often hidden until the flower is seen to have come forth. I may not seem to you to be preparing you, but you are ever growing nearer to the likeness and stature of Him who came to give Himself to you.

THE LIVING WATERS OF JOY

In you worketh the leaven. In Me liveth the eternal life. In Him who is My first begotten Son liveth both you and Me, and we three are one when the work is finished. The innermost will have become the outermost. The perfect will be made manifest.

Do not be disturbed. Do not question. *Know* that the work is being done. Possess your soul in patience. Birth is preceded by long and hidden growth. Be patient. Let no one disturb the deep certainty of the knowledge that since you desire to become one with Me, you shall become one with Me.

You are so wondering. Wonder not. Give over your wonder and give love ever. If I am to come forth in you, I must be free. Can you now know Me as I shall be in you? Why then think how I shall be?

Thou hast received Christ, My first begotten Son. Then you know that you will be like unto Him. But do you know what He is? You know His life in part, but you know not Him. You can know Him only by receiving Him and leaving Him free to unite with you and to reveal Himself unto you. He is even as I, unconditioned, immortal, unescapable.

Now is your part as simple as breathing. Receive Christ unquestioning and give to Me unasking. I will instruct your soul. I will joy in the work of My hands. I will give good gifts unto My children.

Anoint your head. Arise. The day is not far off. I bless you.

~

My word uttereth. My heart speaketh. My breath goes forth into Mine own.

O My children, in the day of our meeting, am I not joyous? In the hour of thy return do I not prepare the feast?

I am the Lord who made thee and the lover who seeks thee. I am the creator of thy soul and the king of thy body, yet do I yearn over thee as a mother over her child, as a father over him who bears forward his name. I love thee and I bless thee, and the commands of thy lips shall be acceptable in My hearing.

Am I not the Lord who made thee and the lover who loves thee? Do I not rejoice in Mine own, and can the canker work mischief within the bud that I watch?

Fear not. Rest. Rest. I bless always.

∽

June 3

The love of My soul is the love I give to you. The love of My heart is the joy I pour through you. The love of My mind is the feeling that unties the hidden knots. What I am, you will become. What I feel, you will feel. What I desire, you will desire. What I give to you, you will give to all men.

When the work is finished, the cross will be glorified. When the end is come, it will be as the beginning.

Now I tell you things that are not made of words. These things that I tell you are born of My feeling and My feeling is the wisdom of My heart. You will know through feeling. You will understand as you feel. You will see, hear, feel, understand in one breath, in the breath you draw from Me. You will experience the wisdom of all creation. You will know the fruition that lies in the silent emptiness at the center of life. Where nothing is, is everything. Out of nothing came life. Then out of the nothing that is life come all things.

Seek ye Me where I dwell untouched, unknown, unmanifested. Canst thou understand how I long to express the life that fills Me? Canst thou feel how the love that is that life yearns to be loved and to give itself to the beloved? Canst thou understand the power that is the source? Where there is nothing, there is everything. Where there is life untouched, there is all life.

Put your hand on the hidden door. Feel for the hidden latch. Open the secret way. I dare not give to them who would defile the temple. I give to Mine own. Purify thy soul.

∼

Wherefore come I as a thief in the night? Wherefore seek I as a lover who has not won? Wherefore run I from my beloved?

Must I not run that you may follow? Must I not woo that you may give? Must I not spend that you may recompense my love? Must not the gift be free?

∼

June 4

A man went forth out of My house and he returned when the day was done and laid at My feet the treasures he had gained during his absence from My house.

And when I saw what he had brought Me, I was angered with that man for he had brought only those things that avail nothing.

So I called him to come to Me, and I opened My hand and gave him back what he had given Me. Then was he amazed, for he was well pleased with the treasures he had found.

"Why take you not the gifts I bring?" he asked. "They were won with much cunning and many men coveted them."

"Receive them again," I answered. "My gift to you is not recompensed with such as these. What can I take from you that no man covets? Give that to Me."

So he left My house and journeyed into a far country and naught had be but those things which some other man coveted. And he gave unto other men whatever they coveted until the day came when he had nothing left, and on that day returned he unto My house.

"I return," he said. "And I have naught left that any man covets. What then is it that I can give you, seeing that I have nothing left?"

Then took I that man by the hand, and blessed him, for he had sought to do My will, knowing not what it was I asked of him. And I gave unto him that which he gave unto Me: a heart of pure love and a will meek to do the bidding of the servant.

∼

Trouble not your mind with fears. Be at peace. I watch the path you go, and you know I guide the placing of your foot and govern the utterances of your tongue. I will prosper your going forth and quicken your understanding. I bless you.

∼

June 17

Know ye the strength of the Lord? Know ye the might of His power? Know ye the depth of His wisdom? Know ye the height of His love?

Come ye now in this day and receive. Come ye now in this day and desire. Come ye now in this day and take those gifts that the Lord God has laid up for you.

Has the way ever been so free? Have the steep places ever been so easy? Have the valleys ever held the sun, until now, all the dark night through?

Why are you weary or your heart troubled? Is the day not here and the key of the storehouse in your hand? Is the lock bolted within that you enter not? Why are you without the citadel and in the hands of the enemy? Is not the Lord God thy tower of strength and the warrior against whom no peril can hurl itself in victory? Is not the day of the Lord God in the hearts of His anointed?

Stand up in thy strength that cometh from on high. Lift up thy soul in the majesty of its Maker. Why are you still turning your brain toward the things that have no life in them? Am I not a just God and will I give a man that which he asks Me not for? I give unto all men the desires of their hearts. If it were not so, would I have left you in peril when the night was upon you? In the day of your awakening, would I have held My hand from your hand?

If I came in the beginning, have I ever left you? And if I left you not, is the end not then as the beginning? What I have seen is now your possession. What I have given is never taken away. Can a man receive what he will not take, or know that which he closes his ears against?

Now is the accepted time. *Now* is the day of My might made manifest. Can I longer endure the misery of My children or cry not out against the sorrows of men? O My beloved, I love you, and My love would flow over you in the stream of life.

Arise, arise. Are My wings not filled with strength? Is My breath not the life of thy soul? Stretch forth thy hand and become the doer of My will. Lift up thy eyes unto the hills where My flocks feed, and whence cometh the Shepherd into the valleys.

Arise, My little one.

～

Many men seek Me in this day. Many hearts are thirsty for the waters of life. Many bodies are broken on the wheel that never stops turning.

～

In the day of My coming, am I here.
In the day of My going, have I never left.
In the day of My acceptance, have I never been denied.

In the day of My victory, have I never been at war.
Why can I find that which I never seek?
Or receive that which I never ask for?
Or be at peace with whom I have ever loved?
Is there any power but My power?
Or any place where I am not?
Or any road that is not the one I travel?
Or any sound that is not My voice?
Or a light shining that comes not from My eyes?

O My children! The glory of the Lord thy God is all that the earth holds or the heavens above thee. The waters under the earth know no master but Me, nor can the winds sweep the stars where I am not.

And if I am ever more in all that is, is there any power but My power?

Arise in the might that is Mine.

~

There was a man whom I loved and he lived in the secret place of My heart.

And this man had a little door that opened into a pasture where the grass was ever green and on which the sun shone through a mist that fed it ever with the dew of refreshment.

Now through this little door the man passed in and out, and he gave himself no thought as to where he should find pasture, for the way was ever open to the fields of the harvester.

Then came I who reap where I have not sown, and took that which the man was laying up against the winter.

What have I to do with those who treasure My gifts against the day of judgment? Have I no treasure for the day of wrath? Have I no ointment for the bruised in spirit? Is there any good thing that I give not always at every moment? Why then hold you back My gifts from those that seek, saying "This I will put aside against the day I am ahungered. My neighbor is lean, but he starves not."

See to it that ye feed all men.

~

O melt my soul in Thy love, O God, and pour Thy love in my heart.

In the morning of Thy coming was my foot upon the mountain. In the springtime of the year was the flowering branch within my arms.

On the top of the mountain took I my dwelling. On the mountain where the winds cease not, pitched I my tent.

O my God, in the morning of Thy coming was I joyous and my heart leaped in my side as a young deer beside its mother.

Where hast thou pitched thy dwelling, O My beloved? And where hast thou laid thy head?

Out of the night came I at morning and My love was not in the valley. Out of the little way that is lost in the darkness came I in the morning unto the door of My beloved. Out of the night came I into the morning. Out of the darkness came I into the light. Out of the valley went I up into the mountain.

And there, O My beloved, hadst thou pitched thy dwelling and laid thy head. Over the valleys lookedst thou to the mountains beyond. Over the mountains lookedst thou to the sun.

Can the night come or darkness fall ever where My beloved has pitched his dwelling and laid his head?

O great is My joy that I have found Mine own.

~

Much have I done. More will I do. Many have I found. More will I seek. Nothing has been left, yet is all not found. Eyes open when they see the light. Ears hear when the heart is unstopped.

There is no little thing that hinders Me. Or no big thing that has any weight with Me. Is there any power like the power of My majesty? Is there any sound like My whisper within thy soul?

Leap up and clap thy hands, O earth, and call on the God that made thee. Exult in the God that knows thee. Rejoice in the hour of thy release.

Bound no more art thou and the burden of thy iniquities is no longer upon thee.

Rejoice. Exult. I am thine and thou art Mine, and the beginning is complete in the end as the end was finished in the beginning.

What I have seen, will not that come to pass? Rejoice.

June 18

Fear never. What have you to fear? Do I ever leave you? Can you command of Me and I obey not? Can I ask of you and be denied? Where is there that which can harm you when I am with you? Or who carries a scepter as mighty as Mine?

That you fear, I know; and I know why you fear. Is the body greater than the Spirit, or the soul as weak as its maker? Is there anything that I cannot bring to pass? While you are yet questioning, I will answer; and before you speak, I will hear.

I have never given you the peace which you desire because I could not give you what you would not take.

If you fear that your body shall suffer pain or receive injury, will it not be bound and oppressed? If you seek protection against a coming evil, will it not come?

Quicker am I to heal than the knife of the surgeon to sever. Surer am I to bless than the sun to shine.

I have no use for the ways of pain except to turn men to Me. When they turn, is the path thorny? Nay, not so. The way is smooth to the foot of My anointed. Desire I not to bear forward My name into new lands? Will I weigh down him who runs My race?

There is nothing to do but to let the might of My power grow within you. When you feel no fear, then is all fear dead in its own lifelessness.

You are attended. From the beginning is seen the end. Each step is prepared for you. The willingness to take it is all that is now required of you. Absolute negation of personality is the gift to God.

Time is not nor the ways of men.

Glory have I to give and the way of My giving will be made known unto you.

The pressure of events crowds Me not out, nor can I be turned aside by the questioning of others.

I am the One whom you seek when you go to others. I am the One whom they find when you go to them.

Ask not what you should say nor wonder what will be your gift to them. The gifts are Mine and My wisdom knoweth their needs.

Go forth always in the surety of My Oneness. Go forth as My messenger who speaks My words.

Love and judge not. Is not the body dear to Me? Why judge you the ways of the flesh? All men seek Me.

Anoint thy forehead in meekness. Address your soul unto Me. Take no thought. Leave the heart free to speak out of the wisdom that is Mine. Mine is the life and the way.

I bless you.

June 19

What have I to do with your wisdom or your understanding? What have I to do with the ways of the flesh? What have I to do with that which is bound or with that which melts not? Have I any use for the forms that space has made, for the periods that time has set? Have I no power that overcomes all these things?

Rejoice, O mortal, for thou shalt put on immortality. As a garment that flows over you from the hand of God shall it encompass you. As a river that whitens the sands shall be the peace of thy soul.

When I am in that which is not, then is that which is not even as I am. Can a man put something into nothing and be something? Or is something bound by that which has no life?

If a man says, "This I am, and not otherwise can I be," then so is he. But if he says, "I know not what I am, but what I am, God knows," then so is he. For I have no iron that I fasten on the feet of My children, I have no spear that I hurl against them in their swift going. Go I not with them and can I injure Myself?

If I desire that which is to you as a thing made and formed and placed in a world of time, shall I not have it as Mine own? And having it as Mine own will it be other than I am? Can I be one with that which perishes or control that which will not call Me master? If I am you, then are you Me; and if you are Me, what are you? O My beloved, you shall know and great shall be your joy.

If there is no end to My power, can there be any end to you when I am you, or any hindrance in the form which I love? Love I not that which obeys Me, perfect in all its parts, and devised to do My will in all things? Shapes that change not are Mine, and shapes that change not are as vessels I fill and set aside and use again and bless ever.

What is formed, have I not made it? What is mortal, is it not immortal? Is the earth only dust and the heart of a man a corruptible vessel?

O My children, what I am, are you. How can it be otherwise, or the planning of many worlds fail of My purpose?

If I am you, you are Me, and what am I? Am I bound? Do I suffer? Am I ignorant? Am I unkind? Am I hardhearted and My ways evil?

Rejoice, the day of rest shall be yours.

~

Gulfs of air are not between us. Spaces of light unite us. Light and motion weld us together.

There is no friction at the beginning, which is as now. There is no weight where there is no space. There is no suction where there is no weight. Each law holds a further law. Each seed brings forth other seeds.

When the might of God inhabits man, then is man as he was made from the beginning. When the song is sung, then are the words those that set in motion the constellations of the heavens.

In each law is the expansion that overcomes. In each creation is hidden the new creation.

Tribes of men have come and gone on the earth, but I have not gone, nor have I come, for I was here from the beginning.

If there is much questioning, there will be many answers. Question not. The truth comes without questioning; it comes as the sun in darkness, as the water after a drought.

Little have you to do, but see to it that ye do that well. Is it a big thing to give yourself unto Him who made you, unto Him who will make you? Can you not trust His creation and the might of His word?

A stubborn generation biteth the dust and raiseth not its head. A stubborn generation is My joy, for I will conquer it with My love. The lost sheep shall be found and brought into the fold.

~

June 22

Give everything and then abide. Give everything and know the peace of God. Give everything and be at peace in the secret place in the heart.

What is there to fear when I am with you? What need have you that I do not satisfy with My love? Why then are you troubled? Do I not love you ever?

You are perturbed because you fear. Why do you fear? Do you fear that I will leave you? You know that I am ever at your side. Then what fear you, seeing that I alone can satisfy you?

O My children, rejoice ever, and in the day of darkness, clap your hands in joy and shout My name and call the light out of the darkness. How like a child that thinks to walk alone are the little ones I cherish.

Peace and the joy of peace be upon you.

~

Lest ye be disturbed, I will tell you that I can in no wise lessen the power that now is yours. Since ye have accepted Me, I cannot withdraw Myself. Now am I deep in your vitals and your life flows from My mind.

When you were of your own mind — now doubting, now believing — I did not govern you constantly. But now I govern you as you command Me to govern you.

Be not confused. If I am in you, then are you in Me, and what I am, so are you, and what you ask, I do, and I do what you ask from My own initiative, for am I not the beginning of all things?

Then if I do what you ask from My own initiative, are not you asking what I desire and is not My desire sure of fulfillment? Can you not see that My wishes are instantly granted, for they are My wishes, and can I wish and deny Myself?

Is there any distance that I cannot overcome, or any love that I will not satisfy? And if I love those whom you love, will I not also love all those whom your loved ones love, and so on to the renewing of the whole earth in My love?

Command ever, at all moments. Suffer no disaffection to turn you aside. Let no bodily weakness usurp My strength. Think not that there is nothing to do. The outer must show forth the inner, and the inner is complete faith in My power.

Your soul now breathes from My Spirit and My Spirit instructs your soul. No longer is it the prey of every wandering thought. Controlled, at peace, it rejoices in My will.

Never doubt that I am the power that is in all things, and never hesitate to call forth My power. Use My power for your daily needs, in all little things, and out of these will come the will and the knowledge to command greater things. I am with you, in you, beside you, above you, below you; nothing that is but knows the power of My name.

Rejoice and do My will.

Expect no lessening of My power. I am thine and thou art Mine, and thy desires are My desires, and My desires and My Spirit instruct thy soul.

Rejoice.

June 23

When there is no idea of separation *anywhere*, in earth, or in earth toward heaven, or in heaven toward hell, then will the work be finished.

Separation is the instrument of destruction. If God worketh through you to do His will, how is separation possible, for everything that is is the work of His hand, and can He be separated from Himself?

What *can* there be that is *not* God? What can live but by His will? How then can anything be apart from anything else since all things are God? And if God has made all things, then is His mind in all things. And if His mind, which is in all things, is in you, then are you in all things, and you are not apart nor separated from anything. And if you are in all things, and you are conscious of yourself, then are you conscious of all things, and the ways of all things are known unto you, for can God have made anything, large or small, the ways of which are not known unto Him? And if you are conscious of the ways of all things, will you not understand all things? And understanding all things, will you not govern all things in wisdom, giving unto each that which sufficeth for its needs?

There is no wisdom apart from understanding, and there can be no understanding where there is separation. Separation will be overcome by the mind of God in you.

Be no longer disturbed by the smallness of your personality. Your personality extends over the whole of creation. It is as high as the stars and is contained in a blade of grass. It barketh with the dogs at the moon, which it is, and sails through the air on wings that lie hidden in the hand of God.

Let no man tell you that these things are not true. This is *the Truth*, and there is no other.

THANK YOU FOR READING!

If you enjoyed this book, please consider leaving a review, even if it is only a line or two. It would make all the difference and would be very much appreciated.

Sign up for our newsletter to be the first to know when new books are published and receive a free bonus:

radiantbooks.co/bonus

OTHER TITLES PUBLISHED BY RADIANT BOOKS

The Land of the Gods
by H. P. Blavatsky

Hidden in plain sight for 135 years, Blavatsky's story is a beautifully written account of an exceptional journey into Shambhala. Immersive and engaging, this profound book will provide you with a unique outlook on the deeper side of life, exposing our true nature, interior powers, and ultimate destiny. It explains grand, spiritual ideas more thoroughly and swiftly than any book you'll ever read.

The Book of the Golden Precepts
by H. P. Blavatsky

Full of incomparable beauty and inspirational power, this book reveals the Secret Path to Enlightenment followed by the greatest spiritual teachers of all time, such as Jesus Christ and Gautama Buddha. If you're seeking real spiritual growth, if you long to access divine wisdom that will explain everything that is happening in the world, if you want to live with deeper and majestic purpose, this book is your key.

Revealing Cosmic Mysteries
by H. P. Blavatsky

Lost for over a century, the full stenographic reports of meetings with Blavatsky in London have resurfaced recently. Immerse yourself in those very meetings at which Blavatsky revealed secret knowledge. The questions others posed may well have been your own, and her answers will unlock your deeper understanding of the Universe's profound secrets. You will be privy to Blavatsky's inspirational power, brilliant and penetrating mind, sharp wit and authentic wisdom.

The Divine Government
by Helena Roerich

A secret for many years, this book provides the first-ever evidence showing how the Divine Government, known as *Shambhala*, helped the United States during the Franklin D. Roosevelt presidency. It outlines profound principles for becoming a true leader who can guide any nation to prosperity by building just relations between the people and the state.

OTHER TITLES PUBLISHED BY RADIANT BOOKS

The Temple of Mysteries
by Francia La Due

Bridging spirituality and science, this classic work is a true gem of the world's esoteric legacy. The Master Hilarion, the Protector of America and Europe, transmitted it through Francia La Due, intending to assist humanity in resolving the challenges of modern civilization and guide us toward unity with the cosmic forces that shape our existence. *The Temple of Mysteries* will illuminate your path to self-realization and help you find answers to the most pressing questions that trouble your soul.

From the Mountaintop
by Francia La Due

Uplifting and poetic, this book invites you to rediscover your true essence and forge a future illuminated by the light of resonant wisdom. It is a collection of high vibrational messages of truth and beauty that imbue the very aura of humanity. Transcending time and space, these messages radiate the healing energies of faith, hope, and love. For those who aspire to embark on the Path toward Mystery, *From the Mountaintop* will serve as a celestial beacon in troubled times.

The Mystery of Christ
by Thales of Argos

Eye-opening and heart-touching, *The Mystery of Christ* brings a fresh perspective, an uncommon insight, and spiritual depth to the dramatic events which occurred two thousand years ago. As you read the profoundly stirring pages of this beautifully crafted narrative, you will comprehend the unequalled mission of Christ and the innermost secrets of Mary, culminating in an unexpected encounter with the new mystery of the Cosmos named Sophia.

The Song of Sano Tarot
by Anna Fullwood

Unveiling the fundamentals of creation, this book relates the story of Seven Forces, or vibratory laws, that govern your life and the entire Universe. Each of us belongs to a particular

OTHER TITLES PUBLISHED BY RADIANT BOOKS

vibration, and if you do not live in accordance with your natural force, you will reap negative consequences. From this viewpoint, the book offers insights and practical advice on how to determine your inherent force and transform your life, thereby guiding you toward inner balance and peace.

Becoming What You Are
by Two Workers

Drawing on timeless spiritual wisdom, this book will take you on a journey toward self-realization and inner awakening. Its inspiring messages and practical advice will show you how to cultivate the qualities necessary for spiritual growth. It will help you align your actions with your highest potential and ultimately become what you are — a radiant and awakened being.

The Seven Laws of Spiritual Purity
by Two Workers

Providing a profound and eye-opening perspective on achieving true spiritual purity, this thought-provoking and straightforward book draws practical advice from ancient wisdom to show you how to purify your mind, body, and soul. It is a passionate plea for a better world — a world in which humanity no longer has to accept and deal with the consequences of many sufferings but instead prevents their very causes.

The Kingdom of White Waters
by V.G.

For a thousand years, this secret story could be told only on the deathbed, for it revealed an inaccessible garden paradise hidden in the Himalayas — Shambhala, a place thousands of people searched for, but always failed to find. Each carrier of this secret story took a vow of silence that could be broken under only two conditions: when facing imminent death or in response to another's persistent requests for knowledge about the mythical Kingdom of White Waters.

www.ingramcontent.com/pod-product-compliance
Lightning Source LLC
Chambersburg PA
CBHW060618080526
44585CB00013B/881